LEAD TO SUCCEED

THE Entrepreneur AND CEO Guide TO

Management AND Finance

David A. Duryee

ISBN—13: 978-1508582236
ISBN—10: 1508582238

This book is respectfully dedicated to the owners and managers of closely-held businesses, whose energy, determination, creativity and hard work create jobs and help keep our economy strong and vibrant. I hope this book provides you meaningful assistance toward achieving success and *perpetual profitability*.

David A. Duryee
2015

READER REVIEWS

Duryee explains the financial management side of a business in a very clear and understandable manner, and the chapters on leadership are a big bonus. This book is what every successful business leader must know and understand about how to run a business successfully. **Brandt Allen, DBA, Professor Emeritus, Darden School of Business, University of Virginia.**

This book is written so that a non-financially-sophisticated business owner can learn how to use financial information to help run a successful business. The breakthrough in this book is that the complex and often bewildering collection of financial ratios that are buried in financial statements are turned into straightforward signals about how the business is doing. Duryee has a knack for coming up with simple and clear explanations of what all this financial information really means. Any business owner or manager will benefit from reading this book. **Charles D. Feinstein, PhD, CEO, VMN Group LLC.**

At HomeStreet Bank we are always looking for ways to offer value-added services to our business clients, and Duryee has written a book that is ideal for that purpose. His explanation of the technical areas of business finance is easy for the non-financial person to understand, and we believe that his book will assist in our ability to better serve and communicate with our business customers. **David Parr, VP and Regional Manager, HomeStreet Bank.**

I thoroughly enjoyed reading this book and only wish that it had been available to give to my clients when I was a practicing CPA. I think that the chapters on dealing with the CPA and banker are especially valuable and would serve to greatly enhance communications between business owners and their advisors. **Arthur King, CPA, Moss Adams LLP, retired.**

Running a business without understanding financial analysis is like driving a car with your eyes closed. You may ultimately get to your desired destination but you rare going to experience a lot of unnecessary accidents and potentially a fatal encounter along the way. Duryee's Lead to Succeed is truly eye opening. It provides the business owner with a no-nonsense track on which to run and in a language that is clear, concise, and easy to understand. **Robert M. Gruber, CEO, The Rainier Group.**

Lead to Succeed is an excellent single-source book. Much of what Duryee writes about can be found in other books, but it will take numerous books to cover what he teaches. Duryee has an amazing talent to be succinct: he makes important points in an easy to understand manner, and simplifies hard-to-understand concepts. This book is a must read for anyone running a business. **Allen C. Hopson, CPA, Financial Professional and Business Owner.**

This is a great book. When the CEO and leadership team understand the numbers and what they mean, they have a decided advantage. Duryee's book is perfect for this and I advise all my clients to read it. Make sure the entire leadership team knows it inside and out! **John M. Colosimo, Business Owner and Executive Coach.**

Table of Contents

PREFACE

In 1994 I wrote a book entitled *The Business Owner's Guide to Achieving Financial Success.* I wrote it for two reasons:

1. A book on finance for nonfinancial type people, written in plain English, did not exist at that time.
2. I knew that few business owners had financial backgrounds, and I believed that this knowledge, expressed in terms that they could understand, would assure their success.

As a financial consultant, I had assumed that a basic knowledge of finance was all a business owner needed to be successful, and I was wrong. What I discovered was that *effective leadership* is the key to success. Make no mistake: understanding the basics of business finance, as outlined in this new book, is one of the keys to success. Without effective leadership, however, it is not enough.

In the twenty plus years since writing that book, I have closely observed business owners who were consistently successful, regardless of the economic climate, and those who either failed or never achieved any degree of financial excellence. Since I trained them all in basic finance, I eventually realized that success must be determined by other factors.

I studied the characteristics of the successful business owners and observed how they managed their businesses and interacted with their employees. I watched them carefully and began to see common traits. I did the same thing with the CEOs of less successful businesses and determined what traits they lacked. It was an interesting and enlightening experience.

There are a few other aspects of effective leaders that became clear to me:

1. They are not necessarily born to lead, but they behave in ways that make them effective.
2. They do not have a particular personality type, (introverted or extroverted, for example).
3. They do not share a common physical stature or appearance, but come in all shapes and sizes.

A CEO doesn't need special genes or a particular personality type to lead effectively. Good leadership is a matter of *behaving* in certain ways, and adhering to the principles that are outlined in Chapters 2 and 3. Anyone who does that can lead effectively. I wish that I had known all of this when I was running my own business. I would have been more successful.

We are about to start a journey. All we have is a canoe and a couple of paddles, but it is a sturdy, well-built canoe. It will survive the fiercest of storms, and we will get stronger as we paddle. You might tire at some point and ask "Are we there yet?" The answer will always be "No, not yet." Truth be told, we will never get there. This is a journey that will last a lifetime, and it is both fun and exciting—we will always learn something new, and, and we will be surprised and pleased at the wonder of it all.

CHAPTER ONE: ENTREPRENEURSHIP– NOTES ON STARTING A BUSINESS

STARTING VERSUS RUNNING A BUSINESS

This book is a guide for entrepreneurs and CEOs about how to run a successful and perpetually profitable business, but if you are reading it prior to starting your own business, some comments about what all is entailed in the startup process are appropriate.

Entrepreneurs typically start businesses in their thirties. They don't know enough in their twenties, and they know *too much* in their forties. They know how to make something, do something or sell something, and they have confidence in their abilities and vision. They have no money, no fear, and lots of energy. They *know* they are going to succeed and are willing to work 24/7, if necessary, to make it happen. Entrepreneurs start businesses. That's what they do. When it comes to running the business, they are bored and want to move on to the next thing to start. They are not knowledgeable about or well-suited to running, leading, and operating a successful business.

Starting a business can be remarkably easy. You can form your own corporation or limited liability company (LLC) online, hit up the parents for initial capital, lease some inexpensive space, purchase a few used chairs, get a plumber to install some sinks, design your own website; light up Facebook, Twitter and Linked-In with your new venture, and presto, you are in the hairdressing business. It might be a little more complicated than that for some, but technology and the Internet have taken a lot of the pain and expense out of the intricacies of starting a business.

The problem is that *running* a hairdressing business is a *lot* different than working for someone else as a hairdresser. It is not the same thing at all, and because of this survival statistics are not encouraging. Approximately 75 to 80 percent of all businesses fail within the first fifteen years. The majority of those failures are not because the idea or product lacked sufficient demand or the hairdresser couldn't cut hair; they are due to bad *management*.

Starting a company may not be so hard, but *running* it successfully is. It may look easy when you are working for someone else, but it is not. This is especially true if you don't know and understand the leadership/management process or the financial management side of the business that are both discussed in this book. Entrepreneurs with a skill, vision, and energy are not good managers. Running a successful business is a lifetime learning process that never ends, and it takes both hard work and a good grasp of the complexities involved.

REASONS FOR FAILURE

LACK OF PLANNING.
This is the big one. Entrepreneurs tend not to be great planners. They are action-oriented people who focus on the tasks at hand rather than one or two years ahead. The three most important aspects of starting a business are planning, planning, and planning. See chapters ten

through thirteen of this book for a detailed discussion on how to establish a plan for your new business.

LACK OF TIMELY AND ACCURATE FINANCIAL INFORMATION.
Hiring professionals to keep your books can be expensive, but handing a shoe box full of receipts to your bookkeeper or CPA at the end of the year is not a good idea and is a poor way to save money. Inexpensive and easy-to-use accounting software is available today, so that lack of understanding of accounting or bookkeeping is no excuse for failing to produce monthly financial statements. Buy the accounting software; pay a consultant to set up your chart of accounts; regularly enter the applicable data; and your financial statements will be available when you need them. This is not complicated, but it does take a little effort and learning on your part. See chapters four through eight for a detailed discussion on how to properly analyze your financial statements. Refer to chapter eighteen in dealing with your CPA.

FAILURE TO UNDERSTAND CASH FLOW.
Cash is king. You pay your bills, your employees, and your debts with cash. You pay nothing with profits. As a beginning business owner your sole focus is on becoming profitable, and profits are not synonymous with cash flow. You need to understand this and know why. See chapter eight for a detailed discussion on analyzing cash flow.

LACK OF UNDERSTANDING HOW TO MANAGE DEBT.
Business owners who have a great idea, great skills and supreme confidence have a hard time understanding lender's unwillingness to loan them money. They have no capital, no sales, no profits, no cash flow and no history of profitability and are perplexed when they are politely but firmly turned down at the bank. Really? Entrepreneurs have a tendency to believe that sufficient loans are all they need to succeed. When sales and profits go up in the early stages of the business, they see this as good. When debt goes up to support the increase in sales, they view this as OK and a conventional part of the financial process. The increase in debt may or may not be OK. See chapters five, eight, and nine for more information on how to manage debt, and chapter seventeen in dealing with your banker.

FAILURE TO KNOW COSTS.
Most new business owners have little idea of what it takes to produce or sell their products or services. Pricing is therefore unsophisticated, and may not allow for sufficient profit margins. Even veteran business owners, who have been in business for many years, struggle with this, and tend to let competitive forces dictate pricing strategies. This is rarely optimal. You need to analyze and know your costs, and then set your pricing strategies accordingly. See chapters six and fourteen for a detailed discussion about this.

FAILURE TO TRANSITION FROM SEAT OF THE PANTS (SOP) MANAGEMENT.
Starting a business is an interesting process. The focus is solely on the founder and his or her vision. There is neither the money nor the need to hire a big staff, so management is largely a solo effort. There is no formal organization chart with written job descriptions. It's simple, everyone reports to the owner and everyone does anything that needs doing. Decisions are made on the fly, without the involvement or need for multiple layers of management or

committees. This is not an 8:00 a.m. to 5:00 p.m. environment. You work as long as necessary to get the business going. It is an all-consuming exercise. It's hard work, but it is also fun and exciting.

Entrepreneurs, by their very nature and skills, are good at *starting* a business, but not so good at *running* one. Seat-of-the pants (SOP) management may be applicable at the outset, but it falters badly as the business grows and needs more sophisticated leadership, systems, and procedures, all an anathema to the entrepreneur. One person can no longer do it all, so delegation and teamwork become necessary. A more formal structure, with an organizational chart and job descriptions, is required. Individual egos need to be set aside as the leadership team becomes more important than one person.

The founding owner hates this onset of bureaucracy, and chafes at these developments. Gone are the good old freewheeling days. There are many examples of founders of public companies who are eventually dismissed as the CEO by an unhappy board of directors because they failed to transition to professional management. Few people are comfortable changing management styles, and for a small business this almost always becomes a serious problem. See chapters two and three and Appendices I to V for more on how to be an effective leader of your company.

The combined result of the above six shortcomings is often the failure of the business. Study them carefully. Don't rely on luck or good timing. Prepare and educate yourself for success in the long-term.

This is not a book on how to *make, sell,* or *do* something,. That is knowledge that you already have or can get from specialized publications. This is a book on how to *run* a successful business. Read it carefully and then read it again; keep it handy. Don't resist the need to transition to more formal leadership when it is necessary—embrace it.

CHECKLIST FOR STARTING A BUSINESS.

You have an idea and a vision. You have thought about it for months or even years and you decide to pull the trigger, eager to get going. Careful preparation takes a back seat as you fearlessly dive into the deep end of the pool and either learn to swim or drown. Preparation and planning are tedious. You want to get going on this journey.

The following is a checklist of what needs to be done *before* you start a business. Make sure you check everything off before you begin. What starts out wrong usually ends up wrong, and following these steps can help to ensure that you start out right.

WRITE YOUR BUSINESS PLAN.
If you don't know how to do it, read this book or any of the multitude of books that are available on this subject. Google "business plan" and you will find more material than you can possibly absorb. Do your homework. Get assistance from people you trust. Go to the Small Business Association (SBA) and get free consulting from retired business executives who have knowledge and experience that you lack. This is the first and most important step in starting

a business. See chapters ten through thirteen for detailed information on how to write a business plan.

DETERMINE YOUR FINANCIAL REQUIREMENTS.

This is part of the business plan, but it needs special mention. How soon will you break-even (where sales are at least equal to, or greater than expenses), and how much will you lose before you do? Refer to chapter fourteen for a discussion on this. Calculating your break-even sales will help you to determine how much money you are going to need to start the business. Then you need to figure out where it is going to come from.

Optimism usually prevails in this process, but the rule-of-thumb is that *it usually takes twice as long and twice as much money to achieve your optimistic forecasts*. Plan for this at the outset. Think about the worst-case scenario.

Initial capital is probably going to have to come from your savings, money you raise by selling or mortgaging your home, money you borrow from friends and family, and a lot of "sweat equity." Do not think that traditional sources of equity or debt are going to be available to you. Maybe they will be, but hope for the best and plan for the worst.

Raising money through an angel investor or venture capitalist is beyond the scope of this book, but if you are planning to go that route you need experienced legal and financial advice. You can wind up with significant financial liabilities if this is not done correctly. It is *not* a do-it-yourself project.

Remember the four Fs in searching for start-up money: **F**ounders, **F**amily, **F**riends, and **F**ools. Look for money in that order, and please, if you have aging parents, do not ask them for a loan. It is not a time in their lives when they should be risking money on something with a 75 percent chance of failing.

COMPLETE THE LEGAL REQUIREMENTS.

Your choice for the form of your business is realistically limited to a *C* corporation; an *S* corporation; or a limited liability company (LLC). Other options include a partnership or sole proprietorship, but these forms do not limit the liability of the owners to the same extent as a corporation or LLC. Each form of business has pros and cons, so do your homework to determine what is best for your business. Make sure the proposed name of your company is available, and register it with the secretary of state where you live. Get federal and state tax ID numbers and the necessary business licenses and permits. Do your research on what is required and consult an experienced business attorney for advice.

Make sure you have appropriate articles of incorporation, bylaws, operating agreements and/or shareholder agreements. Know and understand what they say. If you don't understand parts of these documents, keep asking questions until you do. There may be a dizzying amount of fine print or boiler plate that appears to be benign, but it is important for you to have a good grasp of the legal foundation of your company and understand what these documents contain. Take the time to go over them thoroughly and ask enough questions to make sure you understand what they say.

You should know and understand your legal responsibilities as an employer, especially your payroll tax and medical insurance responsibilities. Open the necessary bank accounts. There is a lot of information available on all of this but it is not necessarily your expertise. Invest in the advice of a good lawyer and CPA at the outset. It is part of the start-up capital that you require.

WRITE YOUR MARKETING PLAN.
Who are you going to sell to and how? How big is the market? Who are your competitors? What are the opportunities for growth? What is your market niche? What, if any, is your competitive advantage? What is your pricing strategy? What marketing material are you going to need, who is going to design it, and how much will it cost? What is your advertising plan? If you are sales oriented this all may come easily for you. If not, get some help. It is part of the start-up capital that you require.

ESTABLISH YOUR EQUIPMENT NEEDS.
What furniture, equipment and vehicles will you need? How much will this cost? Don't overlook things like computers and phone systems. Research this carefully and make sure that the equipment you plan to acquire is satisfactory for your needs.

ESTABLISH YOUR STAFFING PLAN.
Who will you need? When? What will you have to pay? What training will they need and who will do it? How will they be managed and by whom?

ESTABLISH YOUR PRODUCTION PLAN.
Who, when, where and how?

PLAN FOR THE WORST.
What are the things that can go wrong? What are the risk factors? What are the soft spots in your plan? What are the reasons why you should abandon this project? This is the opposite thinking of anyone who has ever started a business. Entrepreneurs are optimistic people who believe that they will not fail. That nothing can go wrong. That you cannot help but succeed. Optimism overflows. Confidence is supreme. This is all good, but don't avoid trying to find the weak points in your plan. Carefully examine *all* of the potential risks and what might go wrong. Hope for the best and plan for the worst.

SUMMARY

Hopefully you will beat the odds and succeed, but a wise person considers all contingencies. I remember investing in a "sure thing" some years ago—a "no-brainer" as they say. Five years later and facing huge personal liabilities and possible financial ruin, I realized that a sure thing does not exist. Every venture has risk factors, and you should spare no effort to determine what they might be for your start-up venture.

Thankfully, I escaped my "sure-thing" investment without facing bankruptcy, but it was a costly lesson in learning that things can go wrong. Approach starting a business with extreme caution, and never think that it is a "sure thing." Remember the statistics—75 percent of all businesses fail within fifteen years. Think of all of the ways that this might happen to you.

Careful research and planning, along with obtaining expert professional advice, will go a long way toward preventing you from being one of the 75 percent casualties. Remember that *starting* a business is much easier than *running* it. Read the rest of this book for information on how to run a successful business. Then re-read it. Keep it handy and refer to it regularly. It is the only way that this information will eventually be part of your consciousness and become second nature to you.

Running a successful business is hard work, but it is also fun. Parts of it can be complex but it is not mysterious. Read carefully the chapters of this book that cover areas in which you have the least knowledge. I have observed that careful adherence to the principles discussed in this book result in *perpetual profitability*. That is possible, and that should be your goal.

So now we continue our journey. Starting a business is the easy part, but you have a lot to learn. The rest of this book is devoted to how to run a successful perpetually profitable business. It is a never-ending journey, fraught with perils, but you will be OK if you keep paddling. Getting stronger and more knowledgeable with each stroke. There will be rapids and rocks to avoid along the way, and this book will show you how to do that. It will be a fun, exciting and rewarding journey.

The next chapter will discuss leadership traits and how you should behave in order to be a successful business leader. Keep on paddling!

CHAPTER TWO: LEADERSHIP TRAITS

LEADERSHIP INTRODUCTION

Effective leadership is what separates successful companies from those that either fail or simply get by. In order to be an effective leader, you need to learn, develop, and practice the traits and qualities of effective leaders that are outlined in this book.

THE BIOLOGY OF LEADERSHIP

We already know that effective leaders nurture an environment where employees are appreciated, recognized, and encouraged to grow and expand their responsibilities. Leadership traits listed in this book such as integrity, compassion, and communication, promote a vision and common goal that are essential to the success of the business. Thanks to Scott M. Julien, author of *What Every Leader Needs to Know-7 Essential Leadership Secrets* (refer to the bibliography), we now that there is a biological reason why these leadership traits are so important. No less than the brain of each of your employees is very involved in this process.

The brain is composed of around 90 billion cells whose sole function is to communicate with other cells and with all other parts of the body. It is the health of these cells that define a person's behaviors, actions, thoughts, and memories. Any type of positive experience helps create healthy brain cells, and stress or a negative environment has the opposite effect. If unabated a negative environment can actually cause the brain to physically shrink in size, and the individual sinks into depression and greatly decreased productivity.

Leaders who create a nurturing and inspiring environment have a positive impact on their employee's ability to form healthy new brain cells and maintain existing cells in a healthy and active state, whereas stress and a negative or highly critical environment has the opposite effect.

Along about now you might be saying, "Hey Dave, running a business can be tough at times and occasionally stress cannot be avoided." That's true, there are times when a heightened sense of urgency is needed, but the brain needs time to *heal* from that experience. It is the *chronic* stressful environment that causes the health of the brain to decline and the eventual result is a dysfunctional and unproductive workforce.

Since the brain is constantly renewing itself, leaders who nurture and create the right environment can strengthen brain health among their employees and heal their brain cells that have been negatively impacted by periods of stress.

Some CEOs I know believe that their most important role is to criticize and correct poor performance whenever they see it. "Why", they ask, "should I praise someone for simply doing what I pay them to do?"

The answer is biological and has to do with brain health. Employees with healthy brains create a positive, efficient and productive environment that in turn attracts positive people with healthy brains. Pretty soon your company is cooking with positive, highly motivated, and productive people. Seems to me that is what you should be seeking, and you get there with praise, not criticism.

Following are the ten traits of successful leaders that I have observed over the course of the last thirty years. Learn and practice them every day and you will have a happy and productive group of employees.

INTEGRITY

> *You cannot maintain your integrity at 90% and be an effective leader. It's got to be 100%.* — Leonard Roberts, CEO, the Tandy Co.

I haven't listed these traits in order of importance except for this one. Integrity is by far the most important trait of an effective leader. Integrity breeds trust, and when your employees know they can absolutely trust what you say and how you operate, it is a powerful thing. They'll respond favorably and do almost anything for you. Trust is fragile, easy to lose, and hard to obtain.

The amount of lying, cheating, and stealing that goes on in business is disappointing. Politics is even worse. So-called "fact checking" is now the most important aspect of a political campaign, and you can't help but wonder if a totally honest candidate could ever be elected. Dishonesty in business is so rampant that business schools now teach classes in ethics—something that didn't exist when I graduated with an MBA in 1969. Of course, you can't teach someone to be honest; they either are, or they are not.

Dishonesty in business reached a pinnacle with the Enron affair. Nearly everyone lied—the CEO, the senior management, the company's advisors (some of whom had taken an oath to uphold the tenets and ethics of their profession). Thousands of people were financially devastated and had their lives turned upside down because of the lying, cheating and stealing. The shady actions of a few brought down a major international accounting firm. This shocking degree of dishonesty makes one wonder if *everyone* has their price. Hopefully not.

Integrity is the core value of many companies, and the owners, employees, and advisors would not think of doing anything similar to what happened at Enron. But there are a lot of ways to be dishonest, and lying by omission is one of them. Avoiding telling people that their performance is unsatisfactory and needs improvement is not being honest. Protecting a family member in the business who is not performing to acceptable standards is being dishonest. Taking the whole family to Disney World when the industry convention is in Orlando and charging the entire expense to the company violates IRS regulations and is dishonest. Having the company landscaper stop by your house to cut the grass and charging the company is not being honest—it is stealing from the company.

About now you might be saying, "Wait just a minute Dave. I own the business, and using the company landscaper is a perk of ownership and it would be silly not to do that." My answer is "OK, it might be a perk of ownership, but it is stealing from the company nevertheless." I have seen owners do this when they have a bonus plan based on the profitability of the business. This is an obvious conflict of interest and a very visible form of dishonesty. Many in the company see this abuse of IRS regulations and realize that they are being financially impacted by this act. The employees might conclude that if the owner is stealing from the company (and from their pocketbooks), then maybe it is OK for them to take a few things as well.

This type of behavior sets a bad example for the employees, and leaders with integrity do not do it. They are meticulously honest and aboveboard in their dealings with the company. They always reimburse the company for personal expenses that were inadvertently charged on the company credit card.

For many business owners, however, honesty and integrity are a matter of "doing what you can easily get away with." It's not likely that using the company landscaper for home maintenance will be discovered, so why not do it, even if it is against IRS regulations? The rationale is that "everyone does stuff like that." No, they don't, and if you do not want employees to steal from the company, then you shouldn't either.

Effective leaders set an exemplary example of integrity. They play it straight with the company and the IRS. They always tell the truth. They say what needs to be said. To put it plainly, they do not lie, cheat, or steal, even when there is a high probability that they won't be caught. As a result, their employees trust them implicitly and tend to act in the same fashion.

Trust between an owner of a company and its employees is a special thing. Workers usually wonder what the owner will do "to them" rather than "for them." When trust exists, the employees work enthusiastically with managers as a cohesive team and it is very powerful.

You will never be an effective leader without complete integrity.

ATTITUDE

I never failed at anything, I've just found ten thousand ways that don't work. —Thomas Edison

Attitude is everything.

You need to be the company's biggest cheerleader, no matter how dire the situation. Let your enthusiasm for your work permeate down to your employees. Whether you think you can or you think you can't, you're right. There is no substitute for a positive attitude.

Think about the inventors of WD 40 giving up on the thirty-ninth try. You do not want events (thirty nine failures) to control the way you think, you want the way you think to control the events (keep a positive attitude and don't give up).

EXAMPLE: THE 2004 BOSTON RED SOX

Remember them? They were down zero games to three to the hated New York Yankees for the American League championship. They knew that no team *in the history of baseball* had ever overcome a zero to three deficit. The manager could have said "Hey guys, we can't do it. It's hopeless. Just go out and have fun and we'll be back next year." I don't know what he did say but it must not have been that, because the Red Sox went on to win four straight games and then swept a good St. Louis team to become world champions.

Attitude is everything.

EXAMPLE: SIR ERNEST SHACKLETON

In 1914, Shackleton took twenty-seven men on an expedition to the South Pole. In November, his ship, the *Endurance*, got stuck in the ice, and he told his men not to worry. They had plenty of provisions; the ice would melt in the spring, and the ship would be on its way. Unfortunately the ice had other ideas, and his ship was crushed into kindling, sparing only two lifeboats and a few provisions. They were thousands of miles from help, and no one knew they were in trouble. On top of that, their expedition took place during World War I, and no one could have come to their rescue because of the war.

Shackleton knew the enemy was not the event: the enemy was low morale. He had to make his men believe they would get back alive, and he never wavered from that position, even when his men openly challenged him, certain they wouldn't survive. Eventually, he rigged one of the lifeboats with a makeshift sail and set off to get help from a small whaling station over one thousand treacherous miles away, with nothing to navigate with but a sextant.

Shackleton looked each of his men in the eye and said, "Trust me. You are going to survive, and I will bring you all home alive." Eighteen months later, he returned to rescue his men, and he got every single one of them home alive. It was one of the most extraordinary feats of leadership in recorded history (see the bibliography for a book about this compelling feat). The next time you think you're in a tough situation, think about Sir Shackleton.

Attitude is everything.

Lou Piniella, successful Major League Baseball manager said it this way:

> *It's easier to lose than it is to win. Winning is difficult. Everyone wants to win. It's just that every person, when they're not winning, doesn't want to dig a little deeper, play a little harder, a little smarter. Winning is an attitude, and what you have to do is develop an attitude for your team that winning is the most important thing. You look at teams that win—all the players are successful. It's all tied together.*

Develop an attitude for your team that winning (being successful) is the most important thing. Never deviate from this.

When the odds against you are a million to one, focus on the one. Aaron Baker, quadriplegic who learned to walk and run again.

Attitude is everything.

COURAGE

Courage is doing the things that you are afraid to do. There can be no courage unless you are scared.— Eddie Rickenbacker, army aviator and Medal of Honor winner.

It takes courage to be in business. Every day you get up and put your financial well-being on the line. If you carry freight, every time you send a truck out on the road you are one disastrous accident away from losing everything. If you are a carpet cleaner, every day that you put employees in people's homes you hope that they will act appropriately and not cause you great financial liability. Your employees need to look at you and see a calm and steady hand at the helm, especially when times get tough.

A friend of mine lost his father when he was twenty-two. His mother valiantly attempted to run the business, but after a number of months realized that she was unable to manage it and asked her son to come home from college and take over. Prior to this, his experience consisted of helping out in the warehouse and making sure the parking lot was clean. Suddenly, at twenty-three, he was the president and CEO of a two-million dollar business.

When I met him, thirty years later, I asked if he was ever scared. He said, "Scared? I used to close the office door and cry. I was petrified." He left that crying for the privacy of his office, and he faced the things that he was afraid of courageously and ran a successful business, step-by-step.

Courage means doing things that are tough to do, like letting go of a loyal and well-liked employee who has worked at the company for twenty-five years and is no longer capable of handling the complexities of modern technology. Courage is sitting down with a son who does not have the right work ethic or aptitude and telling him he can no longer work in the family business. These things are hard to do and take courage.

Effective leaders are tough, but not mean. They show compassion while demanding good performance. They are quicker to compliment than to criticize, and they have a high tolerance for both giving and receiving pain. Letting people go is not a pleasant thing to do and most managers procrastinate performing this task, sometimes for years. Effective leaders have the courage to face these types of situations when they arise and take appropriate action.

Effective leaders have courage to do the right thing, courage to say what is necessary, courage to put it all on the line every day and stick with it. Like most heroes, these leaders do not see themselves as having great courage, but it is a strong aspect of their character.

VISION

A good hockey player plays the puck where it is. A great hockey player plays the puck where it is going to be. —Wayne Gretsky

Great leaders have a great vision. You cannot achieve anything of significance unless you visualize it first. No wood carver ever carved a beautiful sculpture without visualizing it first. This is the primary reason that I can't carve a sculpture. I can't "see" it. Without a vision for your company, there is no direction. No one understands what you're trying to do and how they might help you.

Every company should have a vision statement that describes what the company is going to look like in two or three years. It should be informative and to the point, such as:

By the end of 20X6, Durson Distributors will be a well-diversified company doing $5.5 million in sales and operating out of two locations.

Not long ago, I helped a CEO and his leadership team craft a vision statement for their company. It took about three hours, and when it was finished I asked him where he was going to post it. "Oh," he said, "I'm not going to post it anywhere. If I did, everyone would know if it didn't come true, and I don't want to risk that." He didn't understand the benefit of having and sharing a vision for the company with his employees. After discussing it further and realizing the benefits of a shared vision, he agreed to post it in the foyer, conference room, lunch room and warehouse for all to see.

Once you complete the vision statement, you need to convert it into a concrete plan. You need to set goals and objectives for key management and, using the techniques in this book, project the financial statements. Planning for the future and setting goals are important aspects of effective leadership.

Great leaders have a great vision. Make sure you articulate your vision and communicate it to all of your employees. Publish your vision statement in your newsletter and display it on your intranet, website, and post it throughout your company. Make sure everyone sees what you see. In this fashion, they will be focused and motivated and be in the best position to determine how they can help you make the vision come true.

A leader must provide a vision—clear and achievable 'big ideas' combined in a strategic concept— and communicate those ideas throughout the entire organization and to all other stakeholders. — General David Petraeus

COMPASSION

I don't care how much you know until I know how much you care. —Steve Covey, *7 Habits of Highly Effective People*

Effective leaders have great compassion and demonstrate this often to their employees. When they learn that one of them has a critically ill spouse, as an example, they make a point of stopping by their workplace and asking how that spouse is getting along. They congratulate employees on their kid's soccer championship or other similar achievements. They tell them how much they appreciate the work they do. They honor them on important anniversaries. They frequently say thank you.

One of my employees once stopped me in the hall and said, "Dave, I just thought you might like to know that today is my tenth anniversary with the company."

I was surprised and taken aback, and I mumbled something inane, like, "Thank you so much." As I walked away, I wondered why in the world she had to tell me that instead of the other way around. It was the last time something like that happened. I made it a point to know exactly when important employee anniversaries came up, and then I recognized and thanked them for their dedication.

A CEO of a successful company once told me that in the middle of the peak season, when everyone was frazzled, exhausted, and working long hours, he loaded the women in his office into the back of a limousine at one o'clock on Friday with several bottles of champagne and sent them to a spa for an afternoon of facials, pedicures, and massages. The limo waited to take them home afterward, as he had already delivered their cars home for them. I don't know how many of those women had ever sipped champagne in the back of a limousine before, but my guess is that they will never forget it.

Is it a coincidence that his company is very successful? I don't think so. He cared about his staff. They knew it and worked hard for him.

COMMUNICATION

Developing excellent communication skills is absolutely essential to effective leadership. The leader must be able to share knowledge and ideas to transmit a sense of urgency and enthusiasm to others. If a leader can't get a message across clearly and motivate others to act on it, then having a message doesn't even matter. —Gilbert Amelio, CEO, National Semiconductor Corporation.

Effective leaders are good communicators. They talk to people, and they listen attentively. If something needs to be said, they say it. Criticism is offered in a straightforward but constructive manner. Praise and compliments are offered freely and often. If leaders need help, advice or suggestions, they ask for it. Recognition of significant achievements and important anniversaries is part of the culture of the company.

There are many ways that communication can take place today:

- Intranet
- Electronic newsletter
- Video conferencing
- Conference calls
- Regular company staff meetings

There are also very effective administrative tools that enhance communication including: a formal employee review, employee satisfaction index, upstream evaluations, open book management, business review, employee orientation, management succession planning, advisory board, and an employee recognition program.

EMPLOYEE REVIEW

I recently asked a CEO if everyone in the company received a formal employee review at least annually. His response was that, because of the tough times in the company, they had not been able to give any raises for several years, and so they had suspended formal reviews. Bad idea. People need and deserve to know how they are doing. You can separate the employee review from compensation. Employee reviews should follow a prescribed format that allows for employee feedback. They should be signed and placed in the employee's personnel file.

It is tempting to put something like this off. It takes time and might be unpleasant, but it needs to be done. I have seen poor performance overlooked for *years* until the employee is finally terminated. This should never happen. If performance is poor, the employee needs and deserves to know this and be given a chance to improve. Clear and specific performance expectations need to be established in order to maintain employment. It then becomes the employee's choice to meet these expectations. In the many years that I ran a business, I rarely had to fire anyone. I simply told them what the performance expectations were and then it was their decision: either perform accordingly or leave.

EMPLOYEE SATISFACTION INDEX

A recent poll indicated that as many as 70 percent of workers disliked their job. I do not believe that is because 70 percent of all jobs are unpleasant. I believe it is due to a clear failure of leadership.

Obviously all business owners want their employees to enjoy working for them. If they don't enjoy their job the result will be constant and costly employee turnover. So why not ask them how they feel? When I ran a company, I designed an employee questionnaire that rated important aspects of working at the company on a scale of one to ten (see appendix I). There were ten questions, so the maximum score was one hundred. My goal was to score at least a *nine* on each question. Responses were strictly confidential, and results were published and discussed at a staff meeting, along with all comments, both positive and negative.

Most CEOs think that this is a good idea but balk at including the following: "I feel that my compensation is fair and competitive." They absolutely do not want to ask a question like that. No way. They know the answer will be negative, so why stir things up? Notice, however, that the question is not whether the employee feels that their pay is "enough." It is whether they feel that it is "fair and competitive." If you want to have satisfied and happy employees, they need to feel that their compensation is at least as much as they could get elsewhere and that it is commensurate with their duties and experience.

I always wanted to have exceptional employees, and so I wanted their compensation to *exceed* what they could get elsewhere. It was important to me that they felt they were fairly compensated, and if not, I asked them what evidence they had to the contrary. I administered this survey twice a year and always worked on the areas where we scored low.

One unexpected result of the survey was that there were always a few employees who were very unhappy. Their answers were in stark contrast to the rest of the group, and I surmised from this that they needed to seek employment elsewhere.

If you want your employees to enjoy working for you, then ask them if they do. It is a way to communicate with them and to indicate that you care about their feelings.

UPSTREAM EVALUATION

Another tool that we used in my company was the upstream evaluation (see Appendix II). It was an opportunity for employees to rate their supervisor on a strictly confidential basis. Most business owners don't want to do this, and most supervisors find the idea threatening. However, this is a very effective communication tool and a great way for supervisors to discover areas where they can improve their management skills.

I always published the results of my evaluation to my staff, thanked them for responding, and promised to work on the areas where my scores needed improvement. Comments were always respectful and constructive. Employees *wanted* to have a good relationship with me and appreciated the opportunity to express how it might be improved.

The upstream evaluation is an excellent learning tool for becoming a better leader and an effective way to communicate with your employees. If you implement it throughout the company, all the members of your leadership team will be more effective leaders and better communicators.

OPEN BOOK MANAGEMENT

Over the last thirty years as a business consultant, I have observed that the companies that shared the most financial information were the most successful. Despite this evidence, there is a strong feeling among business owners that this is a bad idea and that only bad things can come from it. It goes something like this: "If my employees ever found out how much the company makes, they would immediately want raises." Perhaps they would, but we need to carefully examine this statement and the underlying philosophy it implies.

First of all, it assumes that employees are incapable of understanding that business owners need to make a satisfactory returns on their investments, which is both commensurate with the risk and sufficient to provide for growth and continuity of the business. Most employees have a 401(k) or some sort of investment, and they understand return on investment. With sufficient education, they won't resent the profit that accrues to the owner of the business; they will welcome and support it.

Second, employees want to belong to a winning team, and they understand that the more the business makes, the more they will make (and that the reverse is true as well). If they are at least generally aware of how well the company is doing, they are in a much better position to see how they can help make it even more successful.

Third, it assumes that the business owner isn't paying a fair and competitive wage and uses secrecy of the company's profitability to foster this practice. No good can come from that. Finally, and most important, it does not recognize the fact that, in the absence of specific knowledge to the contrary, employees *always* assume that the business owner makes much more and is far wealthier than is actually the case. They see the Mercedes and the home in the gated community and the country club membership and believe that the business owner is wealthy beyond imagination.

For all these reasons, it would behoove business owners to practice open-book management. Establish a bonus program based on the profitability of the business, and publish results regularly to show progress. The result is that employees have a laser-beam focus on the bottom line and are constantly thinking about how they can help make it better. They realize they will share in the rewards for working hard and minimizing expenses, and they will have little patience for employees who are not carrying their weight. Eventually, your entire company will be populated with educated and motivated employees who all have the same goal— maximizing the profitability of your business. This, it seems to me, is exactly what you want to be the case.

Secrecy in business is a philosophy that has been passed down from previous generations, and it dies hard, but die it should. Business owners who share the most are the most successful. See the bibliography entry of the book *The Great Game of Business* for more information on this topic.

BUSINESS REVIEW

I have developed a series of checklists that, if implemented, reflect a well-run and highly successful company. I call it the Business Review (see Appendix III). This tool examines six critical areas of a business:

1. Management
2. Finance
3. Sales
4. Production
5. Warehouse
6. Risk management

Thanks largely to Allen Hopson, president of Weathers Moving & Distribution, Excel-based software has been developed that allows for up to twelve people to complete this form and rank your business in the above seven areas. An Excel template is available to complete the Business Review. Download it from my website at www.leadtosucceed.biz .

Once the review has been done, the CEO should discuss the results with those who participated and especially explore those areas that scored lower. Areas that need improvement should be prioritized and turned to goals for improvement within a specified period of time.

The Business Review is essentially a recipe for operating a successful company. Set your sights on excellence and work to score over 90 percent in each category.

EMPLOYEE ORIENTATION

You only get one chance to make a good first impression, and a formal orientation program should be in place for all new hires. This is the time to carefully go over the employee handbook and make sure they know the important policies of your company, your core values, vision, and mission statement. The CEO should personally describe the history of the company and its operations and his or her vision for the future. New hires should be given a tour of the facilities and introduced to all key managers. Office workers should be taken out in the field, if applicable, to observe workers in action and field workers should sit with various office employees for a day. This program should describe the culture of the company and set the tone for what it means to be an effective employee.

MANAGEMENT SUCCESSION

A closely-held business can be devastated if the owner and CEO suddenly and unexpectedly passes away. In many instances, heirs and survivors are unknowledgeable about the affairs of the business and largely in the dark about what to do and who should take over. The results of this loss can be mitigated by advance preparation. The business owner should leave behind detailed instructions for what to do, where important documents are located and what should happen to the business (see appendix IV).

All of this should be discussed with the one or more employees who will be groomed to take over in the sudden absence of the owner. A discussion about death is never particularly pleasant, but the employees and the family will gain peace of mind knowing there is a contingency plan in place. This is one element of good communication.

This plan should be revisited and kept current as things change so that the business is as protected as possible. Most business owners have spent many years and countless hours of hard work building their businesses but only a minimal amount of time insuring that the business survives them.

In addition to the CEO, all employees should be encouraged to think about their career paths in the company. I once asked the CEO of a family business if anyone had ever asked the employees where they hoped to go in the company, and he said, "Oh no; we have family members in most key positions, and we would not want to encourage unrealistic expectations." This is wrong thinking. Every key position should have some sort of succession plan, and all employees should be encouraged to think about and plan for their futures, even if that means leaving for another organization. This is how a company builds a rich and deep organization and is not left scrambling in the event of an untimely death or disability.

ADVISORY BOARD

There's an old saying: "A humpback cannot see his own hump." It's also difficult for business owners to have a completely objective view of their companies. An advisory board with outside members can be valuable in providing an unbiased voice in making key decisions (see Appendix V for a complete description of how an advisory board might be structured).

There are a number of other benefits to having an advisory board. It can stimulate the owner's aspirations and confidence about the business and, at the same time, raise the expectations, performance, and efficiency of key managers. It gives the CEO a sounding board for new ideas and strategies, and, perhaps most importantly, it can act as a bridge in the case of the untimely death of the owner.

No business owner knows everything, and asking outside professionals with complementary skills and knowledge for assistance can fill those knowledge gaps.

An advisory board with two or three outside members who meet two to four times a year can be expensive, however. If this is not easily affordable, then try to form a more informal group. Perhaps a trusted family member or a fellow business owner in your network would be willing to meet on occasion to offer help and suggestions for a free lunch or reciprocal duties on your part. Anything you can do to gain an objective appraisal would be good.

Members of an advisory board are not official directors of the corporation, and there is no obligation to follow their decisions, but it can be a good resource for the business owner to lean on when needed.

EMPLOYEE RECOGNITION PROGRAM

Every company should have a formal employee recognition program for birthdays, important anniversaries, and outstanding performance. This is an opportunity to say thank you. It indicates that you care about your employees and that they are important and significant members of your team. Recognizing outstanding performance motivates employees to be outstanding. Announcing the crew person of the month at a general staff meeting may seem like a small thing to you, but it is not small to the packer who stands and receives the applause of coworkers and a small gratuity for the extra efforts. It is huge and not something that will be soon forgotten.

Employees with birthdays and important anniversaries should receive a handwritten note (not an e-mail) from the CEO. Employees who reach these milestones should be recognized in staff meetings and presented with gifts that are commensurate with the anniversary. This should not be put off until the annual picnic or holiday party. It should be an ongoing program which ensures employees realize that you recognize and appreciate what they do.

It's not possible to communicate too much. Never assume that employees know something if they heard it once in a staff meeting. Repeat things over and over and over again. It's the only way for you to make sure that all your employees know what you want and expect to happen.

HUMILITY

> Oh lord it's hard to be humble, when you're perfect in every way."—Mac Davis, It's hard to be humble lyrics.

Business owners and CEOs are held in high esteem. They are treated with deference and respect, and employees know that they have pretty much complete power over their financial well-being. Unfortunately, they often begin to believe their own press clippings, and lose touch with their employees.

Effective leaders don't need to be reminded that success is a result of the team effort rather than one person. They are quick to recognize others, and it's amazing how much you can accomplish when you don't care who gets the credit. Successful business leaders refuse to take any credit for themselves. "It is the team that succeeded not me," they say, and they are right. Employees expect the boss to take all the credit and are surprised and pleased when that is not the case. No successful company is ever the result of the actions of one person.

In addition to sharing the credit, effective leaders have another important trait. They are not afraid to ask a question or seek advice when they don't know something. Then they actually listen to the answer. CEOs can easily begin to think that they pretty much know everything, and no one in their companies is likely to openly challenge that, even though they feel otherwise. Employees see the CEO as a person of great power, but effective leaders realize that true power comes from leading a great team. They are constantly asking questions and learning.

Humility means admitting when you've made a mistake and apologizing for it, and effective leaders never fail to apologize when they're wrong. These actions do not diminish but rather enhance a leader. They encourage respect.

I will never forget the first time I apologized to my teenage daughter. We had a disagreement about some issue, and, a couple of days later I discovered that she was right, and I was wrong. I debated with myself about what to do. On the one hand, I felt I should admit I was wrong and apologize; on the other hand, I was loath to do this since, as a typical teenager, she already believed she pretty much knew everything.

In the end, I went up to her when she was watching TV and said, "Tracy, I want you to know that I was wrong the other day, and I apologize."

She looked at me with an expression that said, "Say what?"
I said, "No, really; I was wrong, and I just want to say I'm sorry."

She wrapped her arms around my neck and said, "Hey, it's OK, Dad; don't worry about it."

I realized at that moment that I had risen in her esteem, not fallen. Apologizing to an employee may be difficult, but it's an important and powerful thing to do. I don't know anyone who is right all the time, and effective leaders are quick to acknowledge when they are wrong and apologize.

I am privileged to sit on the advisory boards of a number of private companies, and I never cease to be amazed that the owners, who are successful and can do whatever they want, seek advice, listen, and act accordingly. They realize they don't know everything, and they are committed to lifelong learning.

Robert A. Millikan, Nobel laureate physicist, got it right when he said—*Fullness of knowledge always and necessarily means some understanding of the depths of our ignorance, and that is always conducive to both humility and reverence.*

CONSISTENCY

> *There are those who would misteach us that to stick in a rut is consistency —and a virtue, and that to climb out of the rut is inconsistency ——and a vice.* —Mark Twain

Effective leaders can be counted on to have a set of values they follow consistently. This trait acts as a stabilizing force, without which the internal workings of a company can be easily disrupted when faced with challenges. Consistency of purpose is not to be confused with inflexibility; it provides a firmness of character and allows a company to be ready for the changes and difficult decisions that will inevitably occur in the ordinary course of business.

Core values define what a company and its employees stand for and who they are. They are what drive the company.

In my business, our core values were:

P	**P**assion for excellence
I	**I**ntellectual curiosity
L	**L**eading by example
L	**L**ifetime learning
A	**A** balanced life
R	**R**espect for others

These values were posted prominently in the lobby of the business, and I assumed that employees knew and understood what they were. They were important to me, so I asked in a monthly staff meeting if anyone could recite them from memory. No one could. I pulled a twenty-dollar bill from my wallet and announced that I would give it to whoever could recite them at the next staff meeting. When next asked, several raised their hands, and I kept going until everyone had earned the twenty dollars. I had to *bribe* them to learn the core values of the business, but I was happy to do so, because it emphasized that they were important to me and, therefore, should be important to them. The core values were reviewed regularly at staff meetings, and they were posted in a plastic stand on everyone's desk.

It is not difficult for good leaders to be consistent. It is part of who they are. Chris Petersen, a highly successful Division I college football coach, put it this way after he benched a star defensive player for committing a personal foul:

> *I'm just not into stupid penalties. It's not even an issue whether the guy's going to play or not if they don't conduct themselves right. If you don't play like we want you to play, you're not playing. It's not even a decision for me; it's easy.*

Effective leaders set high standards for profitability and performance and overall excellence in all operations and never deviate from those standards. They have core values and stick to them, and employees know that they can count on this stability and consistency in the company.

BALANCE

We have all seen alpha CEOs at work. Their smartphones provide twenty-four seven access and are never far from reach. Their phone comes to meetings, the dinner table, and the bedroom, and e-mails are answered at ten o'clock on a Sunday evening with great pride. These are serious, dedicated, hardworking, conscientious people who make sure to check out the parking lot on Saturday morning to see whose car is not there.

Work is everything to these people, and they know that if you're going to be successful, you have to be dedicated and willing to make sacrifices to succeed. If you have to miss the kid's baseball game or recital, so be it. I have sat in countless meetings with CEOs who are texting on their smartphones while someone else is speaking. The message is clear: "I am an important person, and this e-mail is clearly more important than you are." Uh huh. What a lot of nonsense. Who wants to work for a person like that? What is more important than paying attention to the events at hand?

Effective leaders realize that to be truly successful, they must have balanced lives. Time with family and service to the community are priorities. If the CEO needs to be available twenty-four seven in order for the business to be successful, then there is a serious delegation and leadership problem. The smartphone does not have to be surgically attached to a hand. This is an addiction, much like any other, and it should not be allowed or tolerated. Exercise your leadership authority, and insist that all cell phones be turned off during meetings.

Make sure there is balance in your life as well as in the lives of your employees. Few people on their deathbeds say, "I wish I had spent more time at the office."

FINANCE

Finally we come to the numbers. Most owners or managers of a businesses do not have a background in finance. In family businesses, the current owners probably worked summers in the office or factory and then migrated into sales or operations. Analyzing and understanding financial statements was probably not part of their training program. When they eventually become CEOs, this lack of knowledge results in conversations with accountants, bankers, or financial consultants that can be confusing and even annoying. Without intending to, financial people often speak in their own "language," and use terms that are technical and not always understood.

Many CEOs, therefore, tend to take a fairly simplistic approach to financial management. "As long as the business is growing and profitable, everything is OK. If growth in sales and profits is good, then more is better. If things are not going well today, then they will surely improve tomorrow. Hard work will fix it." If only that were the case.

Financial management of a business is a lot more involved than that, *but it does not need to be difficult or complicated.* Any business owner or manager can learn the basics of finance, and this is critically important to the ongoing success of the business. The key to simplifying this effort is to take it one step at a time. In this fashion, it will not be nearly as difficult as you might imagine. *Inch by inch, anything is a cinch!*

This book will describe how to determine the financial health of your business. You will learn how to analyze the balance sheet, income statement, and statement of cash flow. You will learn how to look beyond the numbers and determine what your financial statements *really* tell you. On a step-by-step basis, this is not a difficult process, and, if performed regularly, it will help ensure the financial health of your business.

SUMMARY

So there you have it, my list of the ten traits of effective leaders. There may be other qualities of effective leaders, but the ten I have listed are the most important. Can you practice only eight or nine of them and still be successful? Yes, probably, but if you want to be consistently successful and be a truly effective leader, you will work on them all.

Leaders are not born, they are made through the diligent practice of these ten traits. Rank yourself on a scale of one to ten on each of these traits. Ask someone close to you to rank you as well. If you don't score one hundred, keep working on it until you do. Leaders are not born; they are made. All of it takes practice and thoughtful effort on your part.

Effective leaders attract and hire similar types of people to their companies—high-achieving employees who want to work in that type of environment. The team has fun, and the company is *perpetually profitable*.

This chapter discussed how effective leaders *behave*. The next chapter will discuss what effective leaders *do*. Keep on paddling!

CHAPTER THREE: KEYS TO PERPETUAL PROFITABILITY

If a tree has a problem, you need to look at the roots, but you cannot see the roots. The mistake is to keep watering the tree. That's not going to solve anything. You need to find out where the problem is first. —Ichiro Suzuki, Major League Baseball player.

Ichiro was talking about a baseball team when he made the above comment, but it applies perfectly to a business as well. Business owners are typically slow to "find out where the problem is" and tend to keep "watering the tree," expecting it to get well. Tragically, it is often too late when they finally determine what needs to be done and take appropriate action. The captain stoically goes down with the ship. It's a waste of money and hard work *and is totally avoidable.*

The following are necessary steps to being perpetually profitable.

FOCUS

Every time I step in the huddle, there's no fear. We're tremendously focused. —Russell Wilson, Super Bowl champion quarterback with the Seattle Seahawks.

Business owners who are consistently profitable have a laser-like focus on expenses and profitability. They set goals and check progress at least monthly. In addition, they make sure that all the key members of the leadership team know and understand how they are expected to contribute to achieving the financial success of the business. People are held accountable, and they understand that prompt action will be taken if goals are not achieved.

Successful business owners spend a lot of time making sure that everyone in the organization is focused on success and the goals of the company.

We've doubled our business in the last 10 years and we know we can double it again in the next 10. All it takes is focus. Gary Ridge, CEO, WD-40 Company.

ACT PROMPTLY

The last few years for many business have been challenging. We have suffered through the "Great Recession," and losses for many firms inevitably followed. When sales decline, the first inclination by many is to work harder. Generate more leads. Increase the closing ratios of the salespeople. Hopefully the decline is temporary or can be reversed quickly, and everybody is urged to do everything possible to accomplish that. Keep watering the tree. Push hard on the string.

This is where the problem begins. Few companies are successful at selling themselves out of trouble.

As soon as sales begins to decline, take a hard look at expenses, and *cut them at least as much as sales are declining* to maintain profit margins. Do not wait months to do this. Do it immediately. Determine what expenses can be eliminated. Question every expense. First pick the low-hanging fruit, like travel, entertainment, perks, and some employee benefits. Look at who has company vehicles and cell phones and what can be cut, at least temporarily.

If more cuts are needed, look next at reducing the salary expense. Sit down with your key management, and make a list of your *A, B,* and *C* employees. You know who they are. The *A*s are exceptional; the *B*s are average and generally meet expectations; and the *C*s are marginal, but not bad enough to be fired. Lay off the worst of the *C*s, and work your way up the list. If sales are declining, there is no need for all your employees in any case, and this is an excellent opportunity to get rid of the marginal producers.

Don't do this based on age or seniority or how much you like them, and, please, do not do it based on family relationships. Do it based on who is doing the worst job for you or who is the least productive. Do not keep people just because they are over fifty, in economic difficulty, have high medical expenses, or may not be able to get another job. Just do it.

You may think this is mean or uncompassionate, but you are not running a home for marginal workers, and it is certainly more humane than laying someone off who is performing well in your company but might have less time in service. If someone consistently underperforms, let that employee go. The rest of your employees will be grateful and say, "What took you so long?"

No one likes to lay people off, but it is part of your job as the leader of your company. It's what you're being paid for. If necessary, reread the leadership qualities in chapter two. *You owe it to the rest of your employees to maintain a profitable company and not put their paychecks in jeopardy.*

ASK FOR HELP

You should not sit at your desk in the dark of night with the door closed and the curtains drawn and try to determine the expenses or employees that need to be cut. This is a job for you and your leadership team to do together. Tell them the problem (which they should already be aware of), and ask them for ideas and suggestions. If some don't come up with any, then consider laying them off. They are obviously not taking you or the business's profitability seriously.

If there are family members working in the company who are not worth what they are being paid, this is your best opportunity to either cut their salaries or weed them out. This will do wonders for the morale of the rest of your employees, who have known and resented the situation for as long as it has existed. Don't think you can get away with allowing marginal workers to keep their jobs without impacting the morale of the rest of your employees. They all see it, and the ones who are really producing resent it.

EMPLOYEE AUDIT

Sit down with your leadership team, and go over every single position in your company. What does that person do? What are the job responsibilities? Can the position conceivably be combined with another position? Is it a full-time position? Take as much time as necessary to do this. Do it first thing in the morning when you are fresh and alert.

If people look busy all day, be aware of the first law of business:

Work expands to fill the amount of time available.

Your employees will always *look* busy. They are not going to finish work at noon and sit at their desks reading a novel for the rest of the day. No one is that stupid. They will make sure the amount of work fills the amount of time available.

Be methodical with this audit, and identify every single person who could be put on part-time or laid off, either immediately or in the future if sales continues to decline.

EXPENSE AUDIT

Virtually no business owner has a clear understanding of what each expense account on the income statement includes. Sit down with your CFO, and go over every single expense account, subaccount, and sub-subaccount. Understand every dollar you are spending. If this exercise does not uncover where you can cut at least 10 percent of your expenses, then you are the exception. Chances are excellent that it will reveal much more than that.

Begin this exercise, like the last one, first thing in the morning when you are fresh and alert.

FORECAST

Assume the worst from a sales standpoint, and then forecast a monthly income statement for the balance of the year. If some months show a loss, or there is a loss for the overall period, keep cutting until that is not the case. Get a plan down on paper that reflects a profit for the balance of the year, and make sure your leadership team participates and is committed to making it happen.

REVIEW

Get a monthly financial statement no later than ten to twenty days (not business days) after the end of the month, and compare your net profit to your plan. If it is lower than expected, then examine where you can make additional reductions in expenses. Have meetings with your leadership team to get their suggestions, and then hold them accountable for what needs to be done. Make sure you convey a sense of urgency about this. Your employees are looking to you for leadership, and they want to be led, so do it.

If you do not get monthly financial statements within twenty days after the end of the month— fifteen days is the standard—then put the heat on your accounting manager. The best-managed companies routinely accomplish this timeframe, and, if they can do it, so can you. Do not accept any excuses. Get it done.

BE TOUGH

Leaders need to lead, and sometimes they need to be tough. A sheriff who wears a six-gun will not live long if everyone knows he will never draw and fire it. Sometimes you need to draw, fire, and drill someone right between the eyes. Of course you don't want to, and you won't unless it is absolutely necessary —*but when it is, you need to do it.*

Being tough is sometimes required, but effective leaders are never mean. This is not personal. This is not fun. However, it is necessary in order to run a successful and profitable company. Employees respect a leader who is tough but fair. The best employees *expect* to be held accountable, and they perform well in that type of environment. They accept being challenged. Once you begin operating like this, your company will attract those types of people, and those who aren't comfortable will gradually seek work elsewhere. *A* type managers will hire *A* type employees, and eventually you'll have all winners working for you who want to play on a winning team.

PLAN B

> *Everyone has a plan till they get punched in the mouth.* —Mike Tyson, philosopher and former heavyweight world champion.

In 2008 a lot of business owners got punched in the mouth. The US economy, fueled by a huge international financial crisis, was in freefall. The country faced the worst recession since the Great Depression and Plan A was clearly not going to work for most businesses. When this happens you need to have a Plan B which is what you do if Plan A does not work. Have Plan B already drawn up and documented in detail so that it can be implemented quickly. Keep it up to date as you work on Plan A. Plan A assumes the best, and Plan B plans for the worst.

DIVERSIFY

If you have a seasonal business that loses money seven or eight months out of the year, think about how you might change your product mix so that you can at least break even every month.

Set a goal to be profitable every month if at all possible. Build this into your growth strategy. It won't happen overnight, but it will happen eventually, and spreading your sales out over the entire year will benefit your cash flow (refer to the discussion on seasonal cash flow in chapter eight and expense behavior analysis in chapter fifteen).

SUMMARY

The most successful and well-run companies are consistently profitable, in bad times and good times, in prosperity or deep recession. They do not tolerate losing. The owners of those successful businesses are probably not smarter, more experienced or more knowledgeable than you are, but they are good leaders, and they adhere to the principles in this and the prior chapter. Make sure that you do not hide behind the economy, status of the industry, or seasonality as an excuse for losing money. It's not valid in most instances.

Grade yourself from one to ten on the actions listed in this chapter. If you don't score one hundred, keep working until you do.

If you religiously apply the principles in this chapter, you will never lose money. *Make sure you look very carefully at the roots instead of watering the tree.*

The next chapter is an introduction to the financial management process. Keep on paddling!

CHAPTER FOUR: INTRODUCTION TO FINANCIAL MANAGEMENT

Financial management does not have to be either mysterious or complicated, but you need to know where to begin and take it on a step-by-step basis. You must be able to make sense out of the multitude of numbers and mysterious jargon that accountants and other financial people throw at you. Operating a business is your game, and financial analysis may be somewhat out of your comfort zone.

This chapter is an introduction on how to analyze and manage the financial results of your business. Throughout the book, financial terms will be defined in nontechnical language. Reasons for performing each step will be given, and it will be assumed that you know little about business finance.

There are two parts to the financial management process:

1. Historical analysis
2. Future projections

HISTORICAL ANALYSIS

The following steps are involved in the historical analysis process:

Spread the Financial Statements

The first thing you need to do is to put the data from three or four years of financial statements on one page (one page for balance sheets and one page for income statements). This is called "spreading" your financial statements, and it allows you to look at accounts on a side-by-side basis and spot trends that you might not otherwise notice. It also makes the information much easier to work with rather than going back and forth between several years of financial statements. This is something that your CPA will do at no extra charge when they prepare your financial statements. All you have to do is request it.

Calculate Common-Sized Percentages

For the balance sheets, each asset, liability, and equity account is divided by total assets. This is called a "common-sized" analysis and it will allow you to compare your balance sheets from year to year on a percentage basis. You will see quickly, for example, if accounts receivable are increasing as a percentage of total assets.

For the income statements, the common-sized analysis involves dividing all expense accounts by total sales. This allows you to determine if expenses are growing faster than sales on a percentage basis (which is usually undesirable), as well as look at the product mix of your sales on a percentage basis over time. Both provide a valuable analysis of your income statement.

Calculate Key Relationships

The next step is to calculate some key relationships that are called "ratios." The idea is to look at what the numbers are *in relationship to something else*. In this way, you can measure the strength of your balance sheet and income statement. What you made in net profit as reflected on your income statement is not as relevant as what your net profit is in relationship to something else. You might be satisfied with one million in net profit, as an example, but Boeing would consider that a bad year. Chapters five through eight describe the ratios that you should calculate, why you should calculate them, and what they mean.

ANALYZE CASH FLOW

The statement of cash flow discussed in this book reflects two categories of cash flow:

1. Operating cash flow
2. Financing cash flow

If you are familiar with the statement of cash flow which is provided to you by your CPA (and hopefully you are), you will note that I have defined both operating cash flow and financing cash flow a little differently and I have eliminated investing cash flow. I don't mean to imply that the CPA version is incorrect. This is an effort on my part to simplify your analysis of cash flow and make it easier for you to calculate on your own.

Cash flow is extraordinarily important in your business, and I have provided forms in chapter eight that are easy for you to fill out so that you can track cash flow more frequently than the annual CPA prepared cash flow statement. You are encouraged to download an Excel template (along with several others) for use with this book from my website www.leadtosucceed.biz. The template calculates your financial ratios and cash flow automatically once you input your numbers.

Cash is king, and you should be knowledgeable about these two types of cash flow in your business.

COMPARE RESULTS TO TRENDS AND INDUSTRY STANDARDS

Once you have calculated ratios for your business, you need to look at the trends over the last few years. Are things bad and getting worse, or good and getting better? What has happened over the prior periods? The trend of your ratios is important.

Ratios should also be compared to industry averages when they are available. This book provides industry ratio averages for the industry of the case study. Your trade association may have data on some of these ratios, and one of the primary publications that contain this data is *Annual Statement Studies*, published by Risk Management Association (RMA). Your banker or your library should have a copy of this publication. *The Business Reference Guide*, published by Business Brokerage Press, is another publication that has some limited ratio information and is available online. If you cannot find any information for your industry, e-mail me at dave@leadtosucceed.biz and I will be glad to help you.

IDENTIFY PROBLEMS

After performing steps one through five, any problem areas in your business will be pretty obvious and easy to spot.

DETERMINE SOLUTIONS

In most cases, the solutions will be obvious as well. They may be difficult to implement, but they will be obvious.

FUTURE PROJECTIONS

Once you have a firm grasp of what has happened on a historical basis, you need to look at the future. The following steps are involved in establishing your financial plan:

1. Project your income statement.
2. Project your balance sheet.
3. Project your cash flow.
4. Calculate the ratios based upon your projections.

THE PHASES OF BUSINESS

The general principles of good financial management as outlined in this book remain constant, but the financial environment of your business will probably change over time. Businesses typically experience four distinct phases, which are start-up, high growth, maturity, and decline/renewal. Each phase has somewhat different financial characteristics, so it will be helpful to identify which phase your business is in to use as a frame of reference as you apply the principles outlined in this book.

PHASE 1: START-UP

Entrepreneurs who start businesses have a vision and are driven to making it a reality. They do not, however, usually have much money. This initial phase of business, the start-up phase, is typically characterized by the following:

1. Lack of capital (equity)
2. Poor, or nonexistent, cash flow
3. Inexperienced management
4. Poor, or nonexistent, financial information

These deficiencies ensure that no one really wants to have much contact with business owners in this phase. They are sort of the "outcasts" of the business world. Bankers run the other way fast, and relatives run even faster. Venture capitalists don't even look at 85 percent of the deals submitted to them, and they turn down more than half of the rest. Vendors hesitate or refuse to offer credit for fear of not collecting what is owed.

Start-up is a difficult phase. Survival is constantly in question, and work is pretty much 24–7. This phase is also called the "wonder phase" of business, because most of the time, you wonder if you'll survive, and the rest of the time, you wonder why in the world you ever started the business in the first place. If you had known how hard and stressful it would be, you may never have attempted it.

Effective financial management and planning are critical in the wonder phase but is almost never done, primarily due to the third and fourth deficiencies listed above. Careful projections for the first couple of years can help determine how much capital will ultimately be needed, and if it is more than can be raised by hitting up relatives, mortgaging the house, and maxing out the credit cards, it would be wise to postpone start-up. A realistic projection of cash flow is essential when there is a need to borrow money. At best, borrowing will be difficult; without projections, it may be nearly impossible.

Chapters ten through thirteen on planning are critical in the wonder phase, as is chapter fifteen, which explains how to calculate break-even sales. Armed with that information, you can calculate how much you might lose before the business begins to generate a profit.

PHASE 2: HIGH GROWTH

Hard work, luck, and determination are often enough to get you through the wonder phase and into the high-growth phase. Things begin to get exciting. Sales and profit begin to grow rapidly (assuming that there is a product or service that people want), and this phase is typically characterized by the following:

1. High growth in sales and net profit
2. Highly strained capital that may be insufficient to sustain the growth
3. Negative cash flow
4. Transition management
5. Better and more established financial information

Since it is starting from a modest level, sales grow at a rapid rate. Cash flow, however, is not good at all (see chapter eight for a complete discussion of cash flow). Capital (equity) has started low and is strained to the breaking point. Borrowing sources are quickly maxed out.

The owner is gaining much-needed experience in how to run a business but often has a hard time transitioning from seat-of-the-pants style management to the more professional, structured approach that is required in a rapidly growing business. Mistakes are made. Wrong things are done at the wrong times for the wrong reasons, and so this phase is often called the "blunder phase" of business. It is in this phase that most businesses fail. They collapse due to poor cash flow and excessive debt, just when things begin to look promising.

That's the bad news. The good news is that you can avoid most, if not all, of the problems you encounter in the blunder phase by applying the management techniques and principles outlined in this book. While success is never guaranteed, if learned and applied, these principles will help you navigate the blunder phase and join the 20 percent of businesses that make it to the next phase. So keep reading!

PHASE 3: MATURITY

This is the phase of business that you envisioned when you started. Now there is more cash coming in than is going out, and you can begin to enjoy the fruits of your sacrifice and hard work from the previous two phases. You can join the country club, go to nice places on vacation, trade in the Chevy for a Benz, and pay yourself a nice salary. You have arrived.

Typical characteristics of this phase are:

1. Strong capital (equity)

---

2. Positive cash flow
3. Experienced and deep management
4. Timely and accurate financial information

Since you have survived when the great majority of start-ups fail, you feel pretty smart. You have answers for most of the problems of the world and are happy to share them with others around the bar at the country club, even without being asked. Now you go into the bank with your hat squarely on your head instead of in your hands, and you expect the red-carpet treatment. This phase of business is also referred to as the "thunder phase." Well, heck, you are successful and beginning to be wealthy, and you're entitled to thunder.

Having arrived in the thunder phase, your goal should be to stay there, and everything in this book is written with that thought in mind. Remaining there will not be as easy as it might seem. Growth is now more modest, and complacency and/or overconfidence may become the norm. As ownership ages, it is typically overly conservative. The thunder phase of business is a great place to be, but it takes careful planning and work to stay there.

A word of caution is in order here. The beginning of the thunder phase is exciting and intoxicating, but entering this phase prematurely and spending money you don't really have yet usually has disastrous consequences. Be cautious about when you thunder so that your actions don't have a crippling impact on your business.

PHASE 4: DECLINE/RENEWAL

Like the wonder and blunder phases, this phase can be difficult. Owners are now likely in their sixties (you wonder through your thirties, blunder through your forties, and thunder through your fifties), and age now becomes a "partner" in the business.

You've largely lost the desire or inclination to take risks. Conservation of existing assets is the primary goal, and younger managers chafe at the lack of growth or direction.
This phase of business is characterized by the following:

1. Strong capital (equity)
2. Strong but declining cash flow
3. Strong but declining profitability
4. Complacent/detached ownership
5. Lack of growth or expansion
6. Unwillingness to take risks

Competition now eats away at the company's market share, as more aggressive firms grow at faster rates. Cash flow and net profit are solid but declining. This phase of business is often called the "plunder phase," as the business gradually declines. A business in this phase can either continue to decline until it eventually fades away, or it can launch into another blunder/renewal phase, which may be every bit as difficult and challenging as the first one.

It's likely that ownership in the plunder phase should step aside and let the next generation take over, but this can be both difficult and painful. No one wants to feel unneeded or outdated, and egos are a problem, but it's important for the ultimate health and survival of the business to bring in new and energetic management.

PHASES OF BUSINESS SUMMARY

As you read this book, think about the phase of business that you are in, and put this information in that context. Many of your financial ratios won't necessarily look great in the wonder and blunder phases, because you aren't yet well-established, but your goal to achieve financial strength as outlined in this book should be constant and unwavering. You want to get to the thunder phase and then stay there, and, with careful planning and application of the principles outlined in this book, you will!

In the next chapter we will begin our discussion of the financial analysis process with how to analyze the balance sheet. Keep on paddling!

CHAPTER FIVE: BALANCE SHEET ANALYSIS

The balance sheet is the first of the financial statements that you get from your CPA, and that is where your analysis should begin.

The balance sheet is a statement of assets (what you own), liabilities (what you owe), and equity (what is left). The term *equity* is the accounting term for the amount of funds left to the business owner after subtracting all that is owed to creditors from total assets. *Equity, net worth, capital, net book value, book value,* and *net investment* are all synonymous terms. *Equity* is the term currently used by the accounting profession, and it will, therefore, be used throughout this book.

Assets are what you **own**, such as accounts receivable, supplies, and equipment. Liabilities are what you **owe**, such as accounts payable and bank loans.

Equity is whatever is left after you subtract the liabilities from the assets, as follows:

Assets what you own	*Minus*	**Liabilities** what you owe	*Equals*	**Equity** what's left for owners

Stated another way, the basic formula for the balance sheet is:

Assets total funds invested in the business	*Equals*	**Liabilities** funds supplied by creditors	*Plus*	**Equity** funds supplied by owners

Study the above formula. Understand that a portion of your assets are funded by creditors (liabilities), and a portion of your assets are funded by owners (equity). The relationship between liabilities and equity is an important measurement of the strength of your balance sheet. The more you rely on creditors (liabilities) versus owners (equity) to fund your assets, the less safe or more risky your company is.

The balance sheet is referred to as a *position* statement, because it indicates the amount of assets, liabilities, and equity as of a *position in time,* which is the date of the balance sheet. This is distinguished from a *period* financial statement such as the income statement, which measures sales and profits over a *period of time* (month, quarter, year, etc.).

CASH VERSUS ACCRUAL ACCOUNTING

Cash-basis accounting records sales when cash is *received* and records expenses when cash is *paid out.* Accrual-basis accounting records a sale (and a corresponding account receivable) when it is *earned* and an expense when it is *incurred.* In accrual-basis accounting if expenses are paid in advance, like a six month insurance premium, a *prepaid expense* account is established and listed as an asset on the balance sheet. The first month of the six month period is recognized as an expense and the five month prepaid expense account is then amortized (expensed) each month as the expense is incurred. Under cash-basis accounting, the entire payment would be considered an expense at the time of payment.

A business may be on cash-basis accounting for income tax purposes (check with your CPA to see if you qualify for this) but should *always* prepare financial statements on accrual-basis accounting because important accounts such as accounts receivable, prepaid expenses, and accounts payable are not listed on a cash-basis balance sheet, even though they actually exist. This omission makes it impossible to properly analyze either your income statement or your balance sheet. Accrual-basis accounting will be assumed throughout this book, and it is what your accounting system should reflect for financial statement purposes. Note that the IRS does not require that your financial statements and tax returns are identical.

The diagram on the following page illustrates the balance sheet. Notice that the assets are separated into *current, fixed,* and *other* assets, and the liabilities are separated into *current* and *long-term* liabilities. Note that the difference between current assets and current liabilities is called *working capital.* There is a strong correlation between financially successful firms and strong *working capital,* and we will discuss how much working capital you should have later in this chapter.

Current Assets	Working Capital	Current Liabilities
Cash		Bank line of credit
Accounts receivable		Trade payables
Inventory		Accrued expenses
Prepaid expenses		Current portion long-term bank debt (CPLTD)
Fixed Assets		**Long-Term Debt**
Land		Long-term bank debt
Building		Long-term capital leases
Furniture and fixtures		Inter-company loans
Vehicles and equipment		Other long-term debt
Other Assets		**Equity**
Investments		Capital stock
Inter-company receivables		Retained earnings
Cash value life insurance		
Goodwill		

DEFINITION OF TERMS

CURRENT ASSETS

Current assets are defined as those assets that will turn to cash within a twelve-month time period from the date of the balance sheet and are listed in order of their liquidity (or *nearness* to cash). Examples include cash, accounts receivable, supplies, and prepaid expenses.

An asset called *prepaid expenses* seems like a contradiction in terms. How can something be an asset and an expense at the same time? This account refers to accounts that are paid *in advance* for such things like rent, advertising, or insurance. Part of the payment is initially set up as an asset (under accrual-basis accounting) and then written off as an expense over the period that has been prepaid. If you have paid an annual insurance premium, as an example, your January income statement will reflect one-twelfth of that premium as an expense and eleven-twelfths as a prepaid expense, which is reflected as an asset on your balance sheet. One twelfth of this prepaid insurance account is subsequently reduced every month and recognized as an expense.

FIXED ASSETS

Fixed assets include such things as land, building, furniture, fixtures, equipment, and leasehold improvements. Fixed assets are always listed on your balance sheet at ***cost, less depreciation***, and this amount is rarely, if ever, a reflection of the true market value of these assets, especially in the case of real estate and buildings.

OTHER ASSETS

Other assets include such things as goodwill, operating authorities, cash value of life insurance, country club memberships, and investments in other businesses. Note that intangible assets, such as goodwill and operating authorities, are routinely subtracted from your assets and equity by the bank in analyzing your balance sheet, since they would have little or no collateral value.

CURRENT LIABILITIES

Current liabilities are those liabilities that are due within a twelve-month time period from the date of the balance sheet. They include accounts payable, a bank line of credit, accrued expenses, and the current portion of long-term debt. They are listed in order of their maturity, with the ones due soonest listed first.

LONG-TERM LIABILITIES

Long-term liabilities are those liabilities that are due after twelve months from the date of the balance sheet and can include a mortgage, long-term equipment loan, or capital leases payable on equipment.

The difference between current assets and current liabilities is called *working capital*. This is distinguished from *owner's capital* (equity or net worth).

Note what types of liabilities on the right side of the diagram finance the assets on the left side of the diagram. A portion of the current assets are financed with current liabilities, and a portion (working capital) is financed with long-term liabilities or equity. All the fixed assets should be financed with either long-term liabilities or equity.

Examine the diagram on the prior page carefully. Make sure not to make the mistake of financing long-term assets (working capital and fixed assets) on a short-term basis (with current liabilities). This is called *misfinancing* your business and will reduce liquidity and weaken the financial condition of your business.

The maturity of liabilities should be matched to the life of the asset—short-term liabilities for short-term assets and long-term liabilities for long-term assets. The temptation may be strong to buy a truck and put it on your line of credit (short-term borrowing). This is *misfinancing* your business and is a mistake. You are using a short-term liability, or source of money, to buy a long- term asset. In no case should you load up your line of credit with the purchase of a fixed asset, even if it is OK with the bank. It reduces your liquidity and increases your operating risk unnecessarily. Borrow long term for long-term needs, and use your line of credit for short-term, seasonal needs. Do not make the mistake of misfinancing your business.

ANALYSIS PROCEDURES

Most business owners look at the numbers on the balance sheet and try to arrive at some meaningful conclusions. How much do you have in total assets? How much is your equity? Has it gone up from the prior period? If so, by how much?

These questions sound important, but they are not. In fact, looking at the *numbers* may lead you to erroneous conclusions about the financial strength of your balance sheet. What is important is how much your equity is *in relationship to something else*. Relationships, or *ratios*, determine the financial condition of your business and are routinely used by bankers and other analysts for that purpose.

There are two things you want to learn from the balance sheet through the examination of appropriate ratios: liquidity and safety.

LIQUIDITY

Liquidity is defined as *the ability to pay bills*. It is a way to quantify whether your business can satisfactorily pay its short-term obligations. Over several years, this analysis will allow you to determine if you are becoming more or less liquid or if you are meeting the standards of liquidity that you have established for your business.

Since current assets are those assets that will *turn to cash* within one year, and current liabilities are those obligations that are *due* within one year, it makes sense to compare one to the other to determine your ability to pay short-term obligations.

Liquidity is calculated as follows:

$$\frac{\text{Current assets}}{\text{Current liabilities}} = \text{Current ratio}$$

This relationship is called the current ratio. It is a measure of liquidity, your ability to pay bills.

In interpreting this ratio, it is helpful to imagine a dollar sign on it. If, for example, you had a current ratio of 1.53, it means that you have $1.53 of current assets to pay every $1.00 of current liabilities.

SAFETY

Safety is defined as *the ability to withstand adversity*. Adversity may be anything from a downturn in the economy and/or the industry to a natural disaster of some sort. Many businesses are cyclical and have experienced adversity in the last few years, and the firms with adequate safety are the ones that survived.

Safety is measured by comparing total liabilities (debt) to equity. It compares the amount of funds supplied by the creditors to the amount of funds supplied by the owner. The firms that have the heaviest debt load in relation to their equity at the time of adversity are the ones that are the least safe and the least likely to survive.

$$\frac{\text{Total liabilities}}{\text{Equity}} \quad = \quad \text{Debt-to-equity ratio}$$

The more you rely on debt versus equity to fund the assets in your business, the riskier (or less safe) you are. Therefore, the higher the debt-to-equity ratio, the less safe your business is. If you apply a dollar sign to this ratio, a debt-to-equity ratio of 2.05 would mean that there are $2.05 in liabilities for every $1.00 of equity, or the creditors have over twice as much invested in the business as does the owner.

The debt-to-equity ratio is one of your banker's most important ratios, because the bank is concerned about the riskiness of your business. If this ratio gets too high, you will be riskier and therefore a much less desirable loan prospect.

A high debt-to-equity ratio indicates that additional equity is needed in order to keep risk within tolerable limits. A debt-to-equity ratio of 3.00 or higher (for most industries) will raise red flags at the bank and cause you to be scrutinized more carefully and more frequently, which is rarely desirable.

Determining the right amount of risk for your business depends on several factors:

1.   Your individual tolerance for risk.
This will be different for every person and will probably change as your situation changes (age, family, etc.). When you are young you may be willing to take on more risk than when you are sixty and need to plan for your retirement.

2.   The status of the economy.
If a downturn or recession is forecast, it would be wise to pay off debt and make your balance sheet stronger and less vulnerable during the tough times. Conversely, if a strong economy is forecast, it may be a good time to aggressively expand your business and take on more debt in the process. Risk will be higher, but perhaps tolerable if no adversity is anticipated.

3.   The status of the industry.
If a downturn in your industry is projected, it would not be a good time to take on a big expansion project and increase debt to do it. On the other hand, if your debt-to-equity ratio is low at the time of a downturn, it could be an advantageous time to acquire other businesses at a depressed price or grow your business and take on additional debt in the process.

4.   The age of the owner.
As a general rule, business owners over sixty-five are less interested in taking on more risk. They are possibly looking forward to retirement and understandably want to ensure that their

money survives as long as they do. This may not be a good time for taking big risks with the family nest egg.

An understanding of the principle of safety and risk is important for every business owner. You should carefully pick the time to increase debt and monitor the safety of your business on a regular basis. This ensures that you operate within your tolerance for accepting risk, and in a fashion consistent with the condition of the economy and the industry.

BALANCE SHEET ADJUSTMENTS

FIXED ASSETS

As stated above, your fixed assets are listed on your balance sheet at cost, less depreciation. Your fixed assets may therefore be over or understated based upon their actual market values. If this is the case with your business, it is appropriate to temporarily adjust the value of your assets to their approximate fair market value and add the difference to your equity. Then recalculate the debt-to-equity ratio. Use caution, since actual market values are sometimes difficult to determine with precision, but it may have the impact of substantially lowering your adjusted debt-to-equity ratio. This is particularly true if the warehouse is owned in the business. If you make this adjustment to help explain your position to the bank, be sure to take into account capital gains taxes or cost of disposition in determining the net value of the assets, and carefully explain to your banker how you arrived at the increased values. This adjustment is solely for purposes of recalculating the debt-to-equity ratio since your books are kept according to generally accepted accounting principles (GAAP) and should not be altered.

INTANGIBLE ASSETS

Intangible assets, such as goodwill or non-compete agreements, may or may not have any value at all, and they will typically be subtracted from your total assets and equity by the banker when calculating your ratios. These assets cannot be foreclosed on and used to pay debt, and it is, therefore, useful to have already made this adjustment before you discuss the financial condition of your business with the bank.

TREND ANALYSIS

Examining your balance sheet for just one period may be misleading. It is necessary to look at the trend over a period of three to four years. Your business may currently have low liquidity but is improving each year. Or you may have good, but deteriorating, safety. Examining the trend of these ratios is, therefore, an important part of the analysis process.

INDUSTRY COMPARISONS

Whenever possible, look at ratio comparisons for similar businesses. It is valuable to see where you are in relation to others in your industry and where you are differ. Is your difference good or bad? Are you different on purpose, due to strategic moves you have made, or accidentally? It is important to answer these questions as you compare your business to industry averages.

As mentioned previously, your trade association may have data on some of these ratios, and one of the primary publications that contain this data for most industries is *Annual Statement*

Studies, published by Risk Management Association (RMA). Your banker or your library should have a copy of this publication.

You will be held in high esteem by your banker if the ratio analysis of your business includes a comparison to industry averages. Virtually no other bank customer does this or even knows that such averages exist.

INTERNAL STANDARDS

Once you become totally familiar with these two ratios in your business and what they mean, you should set your own standards. You can and should decide how liquid or risky you want your business to be and then manage your balance sheet accordingly. If you want to take advantage of trade discounts by paying your bills within ten days, then you need to be more liquid and will require a higher current ratio. Industry averages and standards are helpful, but your own standards are the most meaningful for your business. Determine how liquid or safe you want to be, and then manage your business accordingly.

CASE STUDY: DURSON DISTRIBUTORS

The next page illustrates the balance sheets for Durson Distributors over three years. Durson Distributors is a wholesaler of industrial and consumer electrical supplies. Sales are to contractors and retail stores. Julian Durson, age sixty-nine, is the owner of the business and his son, Allen, age forty, is the sales manager. Julian's wife, Sara, is a trim and athletic sixty-two and has never been involved in the business. She plays golf and tennis and spends most of the winter at their Florida condominium. The company was originally founded by Julian on a loan from his mom and dad and has been in business for thirty-five years.

Durson Distributors is used throughout this book for illustrative purposes. Don't be concerned if you are in a different type of business. The principles discussed in this book are generic and apply to you as well as Durson. There may be some differences in the ratios that you utilize. As an example, if you do not have inventory or accounts receivable in your business, you can skip the ratios that pertain to those accounts. Everything else will apply to you.

Following are the steps in the financial analysis process, as reviewed earlier in the previous chapter.

SPREADING THE BALANCE SHEETS

Placing several years on one piece of paper as illustrated on the next page is called *spreading* the balance sheets, and it is the first step in the analysis process.

COMMON-SIZED ANALYSIS

There is another analysis of your balance sheet in addition to the ratios listed above, which is called *common-sized* analysis. This analysis involves dividing all of your asset, liability, and equity accounts by total assets, which allows you to see the percentage trends over several years. It provides an ability to compare your balance sheet with others in the same industry on a percentage rather than a dollar basis.

Durson Distributors
Balance sheet (000)

	20X1	% of Assets	20X2	% of Assets	20X3	% of Assets
Cash	$154	9.9%	$202	13.0%	$318	20.0%
Trade accounts receivable	601	38.8%	595	38.3%	510	32.0%
Inventory	463	29.9%	445	28.7%	497	31.2%
Other current assets	37	2.4%	39	2.5%	41	2.6%
Current Assets	**$1,255**	**81.0%**	**$1,281**	**82.5%**	**$1,366**	**85.8%**
Gross fixed assets	862	55.6%	887	57.1%	895	56.2%
Accumulated depreciation	(602)	(38.8%)	(652)	(42.0%)	(700)	(43.9%)
Net fixed assets	260	16.8%	235	15.1%	195	12.2%
Other assets	35	2.2%	37	2.4%	32	2.0%
Total Assets	**$1,550**	**100.0%**	**$1,553**	**100.0%**	**$1,593**	**100.0%**
Line of credit-bank	-0-	0.0%	-0-	0.0%	-0-	0.0%
Trade accounts payable	451	29.1%	359	23.1%	300	18.8%
Accrued expenses	38	2.5%	21	1.3%	20	1.3%
Current portion long-term bank debt	39	2.5%	52	3.4%	31	2.0%
Current Liabilities	**$528**	**34.1%**	**$432**	**27.8%**	**$351**	**22.0%**
Long-term bank debt	147	9.5%	76	4.9%	67	4.2%
Shareholder debt	-0-	0.0%	-0-	0.0%	-0-	0.0%
Total Liabilities	**$675**	**43.6%**	**$508**	**32.7%**	**$418**	**26.2%**
Capital stock	75	4.8%	75	4.8%	75	4.7%
Retained earnings	800	51.6%	970	62.5%	1,100	69.1%
Equity	**$875**	**56.4%**	**$1,045**	**67.3%**	**1,175**	**73.8%**
Total Liabilities and Equity	**$1,550**	**100.0%**	**$1,553**	**100.0%**	**$1,593**	**100.0%**

Liquidity

The following are the current ratios for Durson for the periods 20X1 through 20X3:

	20X1	20X2	20X3	Industry Average
Current Ratio	2.38	2.97	3.89	2.60

The current ratio for 20X3 of 3.89 means that the company has $3.89 of current assets to pay every $1.00 of current liabilities. The trend is up since 20X1, and it is much higher than the industry average of 2.60. Industry averages for Durson Distributors throughout this book are taken from Risk Management Associates *Annual Statement Studies.*

From this analysis, you can see that the liquidity of this company is excellent in 20X3, and is improving.

Safety

The following are the debt-to-equity ratios for Durson for the periods 20X1 through 20X3:

	20X1	20X2	20X3	Industry Average
Debt-to-Equity Ratio	0.77	0.49	0.36	1.10

The debt-to-equity ratio of 0.36 in 20X3 means that the company has $.36 in debt for every $1.00 of equity. This has been trending downward since 20X1, and is quite a bit lower than the industry average of 1.10. At the end of 20X3 Mr. Durson has three times more invested in the business than the creditors. This is a safe position and getting safer.

The conclusion is that this company is very safe in 20X3 and is getting better every year.

The analysis of Durson's balance sheets began with a spread of several years' statements, and included a common-sized analysis and a measurement of *liquidity* (ability to pay bills) and *safety* (ability to withstand adversity). Two ratios, the current ratio and debt-to-equity ratio, were utilized to measure liquidity and safety.

Our conclusion is that the balance sheet for Durson in 20X3 has both liquidity and safety. The trends are good, and the company compares favorably to industry averages.

SUMMARY

There are two things that you want the balance sheet to tell you: liquidity, the ability to pay bills; and safety, the ability to withstand adversity. Liquidity is measured by the current ratio, and safety is measured by the debt-to-equity ratio.

A current ratio of 2.60 means that you have $2.60 in current assets to pay every dollar of current liabilities. That means that you have $1.60 of working capital ($2.60 minus $1.00). The higher this ratio, the more liquid you are. Liquidity is important, because it is where you operate financially every day. You need to be able to pay your bills and other obligations on a timely basis. Firms get into trouble quickly when times are bad and there is a lack of liquidity, and it's why some of your customers don't pay you promptly. They lack liquidity and working capital, and they attempt to solve this problem by not paying some of their accounts payable when they are due.

There is a strong correlation between excellent firms and good liquidity. Calculate this ratio monthly, and manage your firm so that it is sufficiently liquid, with strong working capital. *Working capital* is the difference between current assets and current liabilities.

A debt-to-equity ratio of 0.36 means that you have $.36 in debt for every $1.00 of equity. Firms can often operate for an extended period of time with low, or even negative, equity, especially if there are outside assets that support bank debt. Profitable operations and good cash flow management (see chapter eight) are necessary in this situation until sufficient equity can be restored. You should strategically manage your safety so that you are not caught in a recession with excessive debt and low equity.

The trend over several years is important in analyzing these ratios as well as comparing your business to industry averages, if they are available. A common-sized analysis is helpful in determining the trend of your assets, liabilities, and equity as a percentage of total assets.

Remember that the ratios can be recalculated using values for assets that have been adjusted to their fair market value versus their value on your balance sheet (book value) if you have reason to believe there is a significant disparity. You cannot and should not change your balance sheet, which has been prepared using generally accepted accounting principles (GAAP), but you can make these adjustments for purposes of this ratio analysis. This may yield different results for your ratios, particularly if you have real estate in your business that has appreciated in value. Intangible assets, if any, should be subtracted from total assets and equity for purposes of your discussion with your banker.

This analysis of the balance sheet is neither complicated nor time consuming. Two ratios, measuring liquidity and safety, are sufficient to indicate the strength of your balance sheet, and three or four years provides an indication of any significant trends.

The next chapter will discuss how to analyze the income statement and how to properly measure profitability. Keep on paddling!

CHAPTER SIX: INCOME STATEMENT ANALYSIS

The balance sheet ratios reflect the liquidity and safety of your business. They are measured by looking at *key relationships* and not by looking at the *numbers*.

The next step in the financial analysis process is to measure profitability by analyzing your income statements.

CONTENTS OF THE INCOME STATEMENT

The income statement is a statement of sales, expenses, and net profit. It is *period* statement since it covers a particular period of time (month, quarter, year, etc.). The following diagram illustrates the format of a company's income statement.

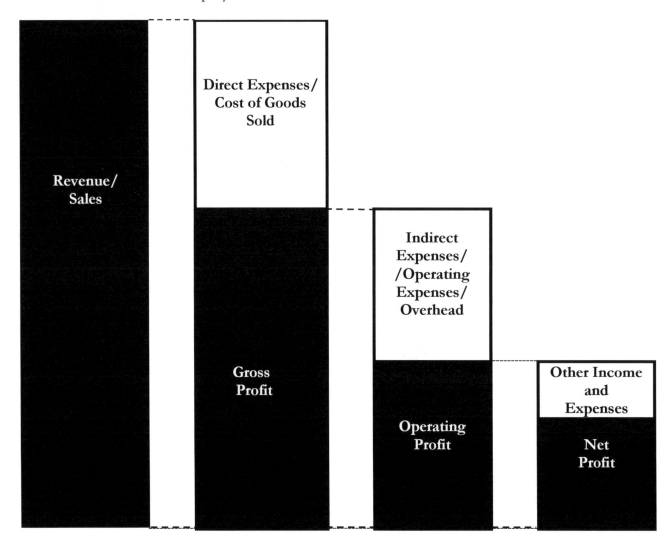

Expenses are separated into direct expenses and indirect expenses. Direct expenses are typically called cost of goods sold (CGS) in a product company. Indirect expenses may also be referred to as overhead expenses, operating expenses, or general and administrative expenses (G&A).

Other income and expenses consist of:

Other income: non-operating income, such as interest, litigation award, etc.

Other expenses: non-operating expenses, such as loss on the sale of an asset, litigation payment, etc.

Interest expense: interest expenses on interest-bearing debt.

Note the format of this income statement. If you are a service business and do not have direct and indirect expenses on your income statement, then work with your bookkeeper and/or CPA to change your accounts to this format. It should not be difficult to do, and it will greatly enhance your ability to measure the profitability of your business. This format allows you to better determine any corrective action, if necessary, to improve profitability.

PROFITABILITY MEASUREMENT

To measure profitability we need to look at *key relationships* in addition to the *numbers*. What you have in sales or net profit is important *in relationship to something else*.

There are three ratios stated as percentages that are used for measuring profitability. They are the gross profit margin (GPM), the operating profit margin (OPM), and the net profit margin (NPM).

LEVEL ONE: GROSS PROFIT MARGIN (GPM)

$$\frac{\text{Gross profit}}{\text{Sales}} = \text{Gross profit margin (GPM)}$$

The gross profit margin is one of the most important ratios that you calculate. This is the front line of attack in winning the war for profitability in your business. If you lose the battle here, then you have little opportunity to make it up in the rest of your income statement. You have simply lost the war.

Your gross profit margin is critical, and a decline of even a fraction of 1 percent will have a significant impact on your operating profit. If your sales are $5,000,000, as an example, a decline of 1 percent is equal to $50,000 in lost net profit, and 0.1 percent of sales is equal to a decline of $5,000. Watch this percentage like a hawk, and when it declines make sure you find out why and take corrective action.

LEVEL TWO: OPERATING PROFIT MARGIN (OPM)

$$\frac{\text{Operating profit}}{\text{Sales}} = \text{Operating profit margin (OPM)}$$

Profit from operations is important for you to measure, and if it is not sufficient it is either because your gross profit is too low, or your indirect expenses are too high, or both. By measuring both your gross profit margin and your operating profit margin, you can determine where to place your emphasis in order to increase profitability.

LEVEL THREE: NET PROFIT MARGIN (NPM)

$$\frac{\text{Net profit}}{\text{Sales}} = \text{Net profit margin (NPM)}$$

The net profit margin is always measured on a pretax basis, because companies such as *S* corporations, do not pay income tax, and therefore after-tax comparisons between them and *C* corporations, which do pay income tax, would not be applicable.

When analyzed in concert, the gross profit margin, operating profit margin, and net profit margin are effective measures of profitability.

INCOME STATEMENT ADJUSTMENTS

Some business owners subscribe to the notion that the best strategy is to make minimum profits, in order to avoid paying income tax. The result of this strategy is that they expense some items through the business that may not be business related (travel, entertainment, club dues, excess bonuses, boat expenses, etc.). The CEO may take big year-end bonuses, grandma may be on the payroll, or the business may be paying above-market rent on the business property, which is owned by the business owner.

These strategies reduce net profit, and artificially reduce the operating profit margin and the net profit margin. In these instances, it is appropriate to add back any such expenses to operating profit and net profit to get a more accurate picture of the actual profit margins of the business. It also may be appropriate to add back one-time expenses like repairs after a flood or earthquake or extraordinary legal expenses in the case of a lawsuit.

This book is not about how to minimize income tax, and it is *absolutely* not about how you can decide which IRS regulations to ignore, even if you are unlikely to be caught. Someone else can write that book, as it is an ill-conceived strategy in my opinion. Purposely minimizing profitability in your firm to pay less income tax sends a bad message to your employees. It indicates that your primary goal is not to be highly profitable.

My advice is to strive to maximize net profit. Be grateful that you are making a lot of money, and pay the resulting income tax. In my experience, companies that worry the most about income tax instead of making lots of profit are the least successful. Besides, under current tax laws, the opportunities for profit manipulation are virtually nonexistent and not worth the effort or risk involved. You are able to accelerate depreciation for income tax purposes, but your income statement should *always* reflect straight-line depreciation in order to properly measure your profitability.

DURSON DISTRIBUTORS CASE STUDY

The following represents the income statements for Durson Distributors for the last three years

Durson Distributors
Income statement (000)

	20X1	% of Sales	20X2	% of Sales	20X3	% of Sales
Sales	$5,368	100.0%	$4,750	100.0%	$4,805	100.0%
Cost of goods sold	3,446	64.2%	3,078	64.8%	3,118	64.9%
Gross profit	$1,922	35.8%	$1,672	35.2%	$1,687	35.1%
Advertising	72	1.3%	70	1.5%	65	1.3%
Bad debts	51	1.0%	45	1.0%	40	0.8%
Depreciation	49	0.9%	50	1.1%	48	1.0%
Equipment leases	17	0.3%	16	0.3%	18	0.4%
Insurance	71	1.3%	80	1.7%	92	1.9%
Legal and accounting	13	0.2%	15	0.3%	17	0.3%
Miscellaneous	39	0.7%	27	0.6%	34	0.7%
Office expense	29	0.5%	33	0.7%	32	0.7%
Payroll tax and benefits	146	2.7%	148	3.1%	153	3.2%
Rent	100	1.9%	100	2.1%	100	2.1%
Repairs and maintenance	31	0.6%	29	0.6%	30	0.6%
Salaries	520	9.7%	528	11.1%	560	11.7%
Sales commissions	145	2.7%	144	3.0%	136	2.8%
Business tax and license	27	0.5%	25	0.5%	31	0.6%
Telephone and utilities	38	0.7%	41	0.9%	42	0.9%
Travel and entertainment	21	0.4%	24	0.5%	33	0.7%
Vehicle expense	73	1.4%	88	1.9%	90	1.9%
Total operating expense	1,442	26.9%	1,463	30.8%	1,521	31.6%
Operating profit	$480	8.9%	$209	4.4%	$166	3.5%
Other income	15	0.3%	18	0.4%	20	0.4%
Other expense	(39)	(0.7%)	(27)	(0.6%)	(32)	(0.7%)
Interest expense	(13)	(0.2)%	(9)	(0.2%)	(7)	(0.1%)
Net profit	$443	8.3%	$191	4.0%	$147	3.1%

COMMON-SIZED ANALYSIS

A common-sized analysis of the income statements involves dividing the expenses by your sales. Do this analysis every month so that you can see if any of your expenses are increasing as a percentage of sales. This would indicate that they are growing faster than sales, and corrective action should be taken if possible.

For Durson, you can easily see that all expenses except for bad debts, miscellaneous, and repairs and maintenance have increased as a percent of sales from 20X1 to 20X3. Perhaps a lot of this is due to the 10 percent decline in sales over that period, but this is the sort of thing that must be managed monthly and caught early in order to maintain profit margins. Chances are pretty good that no one is doing this for Durson Distributors.

PROFITABILITY ANALYSIS

The following are the gross profit margins for the last three years:

	20X1	20X2	20X3	Industry Average
Gross Profit Margin	35.8%	35.2%	35.1%	36.3%

As you can see, the gross profit margin has steadily declined and is 0.7 percent lower in 20X3 than it was in 20X1. That may not sound like very much, but it is 0.7 percent of $4,805 (20X3 sales). This means that the business would have had $34k *more* in net profit (0.7 percent x $4,805) if it could have maintained the 20X1 gross profit margin. In other words, the net profit would have gone from $147 to $181 with just a 0.7 percent increase in the gross profit margin, to equal that of 20X1. That is a 23 percent increase in net profit—a small percentage increase in the gross profit margin and huge percentage increase in net profit.

The following are the operating profit margins for the same three-year period:

	20X1	20X2	20X3	Industry Average
Operating Profit Margin	8.9%	4.4%	3.5%	6.0%

The operating profit margin also has steadily declined by more than the gross profit margin. This means that the overhead expenses have increased as a percent of sales. The ratio began well above the industry average in 20X1 and wound up significantly less than the industry average in 20X3.

The following are the net profit margins for the same three year period:

	20X1	20X2	20X3	Industry Average
Net Profit Margin	8.3%	4.0%	3.1%	5.0%

The net profit margin has declined 63 percent since 20X1 and is currently well below the industry average.

Profitability is marginal compared to the industry average and the trend is declining.

SUMMARY

There are three levels of profitability that you need to look at. The gross profit margin (GPM), operating profit margin (OPM), and net profit margin (NPM) are used to measure the profitability of your business. A small increase or decrease in the gross profit margin will have a significant impact on the operating and net profit margins. The gross profit margin is therefore one of the most important ratios that you will calculate, and a decline of even 0.1 percent should be examined closely.

The income statement analysis for Durson indicates that the gross profit margin is declining steadily, and this, combined with the increase in operating expenses, both in dollar amount and as a percent of sales, has had a very negative impact on operating and net profit. Mr. Durson should carefully analyze all of the direct and indirect expenses for the last three years in an attempt to determine why profit margins have declined and what expenses might be reduced. He should also look very carefully at pricing, and whether or not he has raised his prices adequately to compensate for any increases he has experienced from suppliers.

This analysis of the income statement is neither complicated nor time consuming. Three ratios for measuring profitability are sufficient to give you a good idea about the strength of your income statement, and three or four years provides an indication of any significant trends.

The next chapter will look at some elements that combine accounts from both the balance sheet and the income statement to measure the operating performance of your business. Keep on paddling!

CHAPTER SEVEN: OPERATING PERFORMANCE ANALYSIS

There are five ratios that we use to measure operating performance. They are:
1. Return on equity
2. Days sales outstanding (DSO)
3. Inventory days
4. Accounts payable days
5. Z score

RETURN ON EQUITY

Return on equity is calculated as follows:

$$\frac{\text{Net profit}}{\text{Equity}} = \text{Return on equity (ROE)}$$

Business owners have a considerable sum of money invested in their businesses (defined as equity), and over time this investment should generate a satisfactory return. There are alternative investments where these funds might be employed, many with less risk. It is therefore important to measure the return generated by the business to see how it compares to returns available elsewhere.

DAYS SALES OUTSTANDING (DSO)

Days sales outstanding are calculated in two steps as follows:

$$\frac{\text{Sales}}{\text{Accounts receivable}} = \text{Accounts receivable turnover}$$

$$\frac{365}{\text{Accounts receivable turnover}} = \text{Days sales outstanding (DSO)}$$

If this is calculated for a six-month period you would use 180 instead of 365. Always use the number of days in the period as the numerator in the second formula.

In addition to these calculations, you should get an aging of your accounts receivable every week. To age accounts receivable, separate them into categories based on their due dates:

Age	Expressed as
0 to 30 days	$ and % of total
30 to 60 days	$ and % of total
60 to 90 days	$ and % of total
Over 90 days	$ and % of total

Your goal should be to have the minimum amount in the over thirty-day categories. Over sixty-day accounts should not be more than 10 percent of the total. Weekly monitoring will facilitate this process. This aging is particularly important to your banker, who will not typically use any accounts over ninety days as collateral for your line of credit and thus your borrowing limit will be restricted.

Assign someone to be responsible for collecting delinquent accounts. Focus on the oldest ones first and make every attempt to collect this money. It is hurting your cash flow to have excess money tied up in accounts receivable, which is equivalent to an interest-free loan to your customers. More on cash flow in the next chapter.

Obviously, if you are a cash business you can skip this ratio.

INVENTORY DAYS

Inventory days are calculated in two steps as follows:

$$\frac{\text{Cost of goods sold}}{\text{Inventory}} = \text{Inventory turnover}$$

$$\frac{365}{\text{Inventory turnover}} = \text{Inventory days}$$

This ratio should be calculated on a regular basis because excess inventory hurts cash flow and increases the possibility of either inventory shrinkage or obsolescence. As above for days sales outstanding, change 365 to the number of days in the period that you are using.

Many manufacturing firms increase inventory turnover by using a system called *just-in-time* inventory. Suppliers are required to deliver a particular part at the exact time that it is needed for production. In this fashion they are able to reduce inventory requirements in order to minimize holding costs and maximize cash flow and profit margins. Another technique is to allow your major vendors to store inventory in your facility and charge you only as you use it. This allows you to have minimum cash tied up in inventory and significantly improves your cash flow (more on this in the next chapter).

If you are a service business without inventory, you can skip this ratio.

PAYABLE DAYS

Payable days are calculated in two steps as follows:

$$\frac{\text{Cost of goods sold}}{\text{Accounts payable}} = \text{Accounts payable turnover}$$

$$\frac{365}{\text{Accounts payable turnover}} = \text{Payable days}$$

Accounts payable should be kept current. Late payments hurt your credit rating, can lead to a restriction of credit, and/or seriously impact your ability to borrow from the bank. As above, if the period is less than a year, change the 365 to the days in the period you are using.

THE Z SCORE

The Z score is calculated as follows:

$\dfrac{\text{Current assets - current liabilities}}{\text{Total assets}}$	x	6.56 =	xx
$\dfrac{\text{Equity}}{\text{Total assets}}$	x	3.26 =	xx
$\dfrac{\text{Profit before interest and taxes}}{\text{Total assets}}$	x	6.72 =	xx
$\dfrac{\text{Equity}}{\text{Total liabilities}}$	x	1.05 =	xx
Total			**xxx**

The Z score is a good measure of the overall health of your business. Well-managed companies consistently have a Z score in excess of 5.0. The ratings for the Z score are as follows:

0 to 1.0	Very bad
1.1 to 2.0	Poor
2.1 to 3.0	Fair
3.1 to 4.0	Good
4.1 to 4.9	Very good
5.0 +	Excellent

Industry averages for the Z score do not exist, however the above ratings are a result of my experience over many years of utilizing this ratio, and they apply to all firms without regard to a particular industry. You should use 5.0 as a standard if your goal is to have a company with an excellent financial condition.

CASE STUDY: DURSON DISTRIBUTORS

RETURN ON EQUITY

The following are the return on equity ratios for Durson Distributors for the last three years:

	20X1	20X2	20X3	Industry Average
Return on equity	50.6%	18.3%	12.5%	29.8%

Return on equity has steadily declined over the last three years and is less than half of the industry average of 29.8 percent. This is a function of both declining net profit and increasing equity. This is the *reward* part of the risk-reward relationship. For Durson, the reward is low, as reflected by a low return on equity, but so is the corresponding risk, as indicated by the debt-to-equity ratio of 0.36 in 20X3.

DAYS SALES OUTSTANDING (DSO)

The following are the days sales outstanding ratios (how long it would take to collect all of the accounts receivable) for the last three years:

	20X1	20X2	20X3	Industry Average
Days sales outstanding	41 days	46 days	39 days	36 days

Days sales outstanding has improved over the last three years and is only slightly above the industry average of thirty-six days.

INVENTORY DAYS

The following are the inventory days (how long it would take to sell all of the inventory on hand) for the last three years:

	20X1	20X2	20X3	Industry Average
Inventory days	49 days	53 days	58 days	56 days

Inventory days have increased over the three period, which has hurt cash flow (more on this in the next chapter); however the ratio for 20X3 is very close to the industry average of 56 days. This trend should be monitored and not allowed to worsen.

ACCOUNTS PAYABLE DAYS

The following are the accounts payable days (how long it would take to pay all of the accounts payable) for the last three years:

	20X1	20X2	20X3	Industry Average
Accounts payable days	48 days	43 days	35 days	34 days

Accounts payable days have decreased over the three year period and is in line with the industry average of 34 days.

THE Z SCORE

The following are the Z scores for the three-year period:

	20X1	20X2	20X3	Standard
Z score	8.1	8.7	10.0	5.0

Durson is twice the standard and is increasing. There is no question that based upon the Z score, Durson has excellent overall financial health.

SUMMARY

This chapter has discussed five ratios that utilize accounts from your balance sheet and income statement, and some of them may not apply to you. If you are a service business with no inventory you can ignore the inventory days calculation, or if you are strictly a cash business you do not have to bother with the days sales outstanding calculation. Return on equity, accounts payable days, and the Z score apply to all types of businesses.

So far we have discussed a total of ten ratios that measure liquidity, safety, profitability, and operating performance. Except for analyzing cash flow, which will be covered in the next chapter, they tell us what we need to know about the financial condition of a company. There are a lot more ratios that you might calculate, but my intent is to make this analysis as simple and easy as possible. If there are ratios that are specific to your industry, you should add those to this list, but my advice is to avoid using elaborate spread sheets that include dozens of ratios.

The members of your leadership team should be apprised of these ratios and what they mean, and if you have too many it will make that task difficult. Think about the KISS (keep it short and simple) theory when analyzing your financial statements. More is not necessarily better.

Cash is king. The next chapter will discuss how to analyze cash flow and that will conclude our financial analysis of Durson Distributors. Keep on paddling!

CHAPTER EIGHT: CASH FLOW ANALYSIS

INTRODUCTION

Most business owners strive to increase sales and net profit. They believe that if they have more profit they will have more cash. If only that were true.

Cash flow is equally important to analyze because you pay your bills, your employees, your taxes, and your bank loans with cash. Net profit is important, but *cash is king*.

There are several reasons why business owners do not focus much on cash flow:

1. It seems intuitively correct that the more money you make, the more money (cash) you will have.
2. Cash flow is not well understood. If you ask five financial analysts for the definition of cash flow, you may get five different answers. This is not helpful.
3. Of the hundreds of numbers on your monthly balance sheet and income statement, not one relates to or measures cash flow.
4. The CPA-prepared statement of cash flow that you receive on an annual basis is not well understood.
5. There are no ratios (until now) that help you analyze cash flow.

A concentrated focus on sales and profits is good (refer to chapter six), but your focus needs to also include cash flow. It's important for you to be profitable, but good cash flow management is absolutely essential to the ongoing success of your business. What makes this challenging is that you can have huge profits and negative cash flow or huge losses and positive cash flow.

IMPACTS ON CASH FLOW

Factors from both the income statement and the balance sheet impact cash flow in your business. These factors can be either positive or negative according to the following:

Income Statement	Impact on Cash Flow	Balance Sheet
Profit ⟶	POSITIVE	⟵ Asset Decrease Liability Increase
Loss ⟶	NEGATIVE	⟵ Asset Increase Liability Decrease

POSITIVE CASH FLOW FACTORS

The positive contribution to cash flow from the income statement is net profit. Emphasis is on the word *contribution*. Net profit does not ever equate to cash flow, but does contribute to it.

The positive contribution from the balance sheet is when assets go *down* or liabilities go *up*. Selling equipment or reducing accounts receivable generates positive cash flow. Obtaining a bank loan or increasing accounts payable also generates positive cash flow.

NEGATIVE CASH FLOW FACTORS

When sales go up this causes assets like accounts receivable, inventory, and equipment to also go up. When assets go *up*, cash goes *down*. In most instances the negative cash flow impact from an increase in sales is larger than the positive cash flow impact of net profit, which causes cash flow to be negative.

If growth in sales and net profit is significant over several years, there will likely be an inverse relationship between profit and cash flow, which is caused by the increase in assets caused by the increase in sales. To solve this your first instinct is to work harder and increase sales and profit which, of course, makes cash flow even worse. This is counterintuitive to what you think should make sense and it's called *growing broke*.

TYPES OF CASH FLOW

There are two types of cash flow that will be defined and discussed in this book:

1. Operating cash flow: cash flow from the operations of the business
2. Financing cash flow: cash flow from banks and/or shareholders

You will be able to determine what has happened to cash flow on a historical basis and then be in a good position to determine if you are going to have a cash flow problem in the future if you understand and monitor these two types of cash flow. These two types of cash flow are similar, but not identical, to those that are contained in the statement of cash flow which is provided by your CPA. I have changed them somewhat so that they will be both easier for you to measure and to understand.

OPERATING CASH FLOW

Operating cash flow is cash flow generated from the day-to-day operations of your business. It consists of net profit (or loss) and changes in selected assets and liabilities from one period to the next as follows:

	Net profit (loss)
plus	Change in current assets, excluding cash
plus	Change in current liabilities, excluding bank and shareholder debt
plus	Change in net fixed assets
plus	Change in non-current assets
equals	**Operating cash flow**

Analyzing operating cash flow can be challenging because:

1. Positive operating cash flow is not necessarily good.
    You can accomplish this by simply not paying your accounts payable. An *increase* in liabilities causes cash flow to go *up*.
2. Negative operating cash flow is not necessarily bad in the short-term.
    This may be the result of a growth in sales and net profit, which causes an increase in accounts receivable and various other current assets. An *increase* in assets causes cash flow to go *down*.

Cash flow therefore needs to be measured within the context of the other financial ratios that measure liquidity, safety, and profitability. A rapid growth in sales causes an increase in equipment, accounts receivable, and inventory that could result in negative operating cash flow. If the financial ratios discussed in chapters five through seven are solid and reflect good liquidity, safety, profitability, and operating performance, then it may be OK in the short-term to have negative operating cash flow.

Positive operating cash flow is not always good, and negative operating cash flow is not always bad. One principle, however, can be stated here with absolute certainty:

> *You cannot have negative operating cash flow year after year, and survive.*

You must eventually generate positive operating cash flow, or you will build up so much bank and trade debt that you will be in serious trouble from a safety standpoint, despite the fact that you are growing and profitable.

Without additional equity investment or shareholder loans, you would "grow yourself broke" by funding negative operating cash flow with bank and trade debt. Unfortunately, you may load up with debt when things are going well and then get cut off when safety, as measured by the debt-to-equity ratio, declines below tolerable limits. You must utilize the financial analysis concepts in this book, and make sure you don't end up a casualty in this type of scenario. *Your creditors will probably survive, but you may not.*

You need to carefully monitor cash flow while you are building the sales and net profit of your business.

FINANCING CASH FLOW
Financing cash flow consists of changes in bank/lease debt, shareholder debt, and other long-term debt from one period to the next as follows:

	Change in bank or lease debt
plus	Change in shareholder debt
plus	Change in other non-current debt
plus	<u>Equity adjustment</u>
equals	**Financing cash flow**

Bank debt consists of your line of credit, current portion of long-term debt, and any capital leases that are on your balance sheet.

Changes in other long-term liabilities consist of such things as loans to an affiliate or any other long-term liability.

An equity adjustment is a result of either a distribution to shareholders, a contribution to equity by shareholders, or an adjustment made by your CPA to retained earnings. Distributions to shareholders are fairly common in an *S* corporation so that shareholders will have money to make estimated quarterly income tax payments.

The amount of an equity adjustment, if any, is calculated by the following formula:

	Current-period equity
minus	Current-period net profit
minus	<u>Prior-period equity</u>
	equals Equity adjustment

Durson Distributors Example (000):

Equity 20X3	$1,204
Minus Profit 20X3	(147)
Minus Equity 20X2	<u>(1,163)</u>
Equity Adjustment	(106)

The equity adjustment is negative and that means that the company made a distribution to Mr. Durson in that amount. If it had been positive, it would have indicated that he made an equity contribution to the business.

The following is a summary of the two types of cash flow

Account	Cash flow type	Impact
Profit	Operating	Positive
Current assets[1] decrease	Operating	Positive
Current liabilities[2] increase	Operating	Positive
Net fixed assets decrease	Operating	Positive
Non-current assets decrease	Operating	Positive
Bank/lease debt increase	Financing	Positive
Shareholder loan increase	Financing	Positive
Other non-current liabilities increase	Financing	Positive
Equity adjustment-contribution	Financing	Positive
Loss	Operating	Negative
Current assets[1] increase	Operating	Negative
Current liabilities[2] decrease	Operating	Negative
Net fixed assets increase	Operating	Negative
Non-current assets increase	Operating	Negative
Bank/lease debt decrease	Financing	Negative
Shareholder loan decrease	Financing	Negative
Other non-current liabilities decrease	Financing	Negative
Equity adjustment-distribution	Financing	Negative

[1] excluding cash
[2] excluding bank/shareholder debt

Note that an increase in assets has a *negative* impact on cash flow, and an increase in liabilities has a *positive* impact. This is counterintuitive, since you have probably always thought that assets are good and liabilities are bad. From a cash flow standpoint, the opposite is true.

ANALYZING CASH FLOW

As stated earlier, you need to analyze cash flow within the overall context of the financial ratios, as discussed in Chapters five through seven. And you cannot look at the cash flow *numbers* and determine whether your cash flow is good or bad. This is true for at least two reasons:

1. The business may be declining, and operating assets, like accounts receivable and supplies, are being liquidated, providing positive cash flow.
2. The business may have delayed paying accounts payable, providing positive cash flow.

Both these factors will produce positive operating cash flow; however, both indicate financial problems.

By the same token, having negative operating cash flow, at least in the short term, is not necessarily bad. Sales growth will cause an increase in operating assets that might result in negative operating cash flow. This may be beneficial to the business as long as the financial condition of the business is solid.

The following two principles are true regarding cash flow:

1. Over time, operating cash flow must be sufficient to provide for the payback of debt.
2. Over time, continued negative operating cash flow will not work. Creditors will shut off the supply of money to make up for the negative operating cash flow because the debt-to-equity will increase and the safety of the business will decrease.

At some point, if you don't increase equity capital, your business must produce positive operating cash flow. This sounds absurdly obvious, but I have seen more than one company "grow itself broke."

CASH FLOW RATIOS

There are three ratios that are used to measure and analyze cash flow.

OPERATING CASH FLOW MARGIN - OPCFM

The OpCFM is calculated by dividing operating cash flow by sales.

$$\frac{\text{Operating cash flow}}{\text{Sales}} = \text{Operating cash flow margin (OpCFM)}$$

This ratio is similar to the operating profit margin discussed in chapter six, which compares operating profit to sales. The difference is that this ratio measures operating cash flow instead of operating profit as a percent of sales.

This ratio may be positive or negative in any given year, depending on the growth and financial situation of the business.

FINANCING CASH FLOW MARGIN (FINCFM)

The FinCFM is calculated by dividing financing cash flow by sales.

$$\frac{\text{Financing cash flow}}{\text{Sales}} = \text{Financing cash flow margin (FinCFM)}$$

The financing cash flow Margin is expressed as a percent of sales.

This ratio may be positive or negative in any given year, depending on the growth and financial situation of the business.

NET CASH FLOW MARGIN – (NETCFM)

	Operating cash flow margin
plus	Financing cash flow margin
equals	Net cash flow margin

This ratio may be positive or negative in any given year, depending on the growth in the business, but, over time, it should be positive and average between 0.1 and 0.5 percent of sales.

CASE STUDY: DURSON DISTRIBUTORS

The following reflects the cash flow analysis for the last three years for Durson Distributors. There are only two years reflected in this analysis, 20X2 and 20X3, because cash flow is measured by looking at the changes between one year and the next. Thus only two columns can be generated from three periods of financial statements: the changes from 20X1 to 20X2 (labeled "20X2") and the changes from 20X2 to 20X3 (labeled "20X3").

	20X2	20X3
Net profit	$191	$147
Change in current assets[1]	22	31
Change in current liabilities[2]	(109)	(60)
Change in net fixed assets	25	40
Change in noncurrent Assets	(2)	5
Operating cash flow	**$127**	**$163**

[1] excluding cash
[2] excluding bank/lease debt and shareholder debt

Operating cash flow margin
$127 ÷ sales of $4,750	2.7%	
$163 ÷ sales of $4,805		3.4%

The operating cash flow margins for 20X2 and 20X3 are both positive. This is due to the decline in assets, which resulted from the decline in sales. When assets go *down*, cash flow goes *up*. Some, but not all, of the cash generated by the decline in assets was used to pay off current liabilities.

	20X2	20X3
Change in bank/lease debt	($58)	($30)
Change in shareholder debt	-0-	-0-
Change in other long-term	-0-	-0-
Equity adjustment	(21)	(17)
Financing cash flow	**($79)**	**($47)**

Financing cash flow margin
($79) ÷ sales of $4,750	(1.7%)	
($47) ÷ sales of $4,805		(1.0%)

Financing cash flow is negative in both 20X2 and 20X3. When liabilities go *down*, cash flow goes *down*.

Both types of cash flow margins added together produce the net cash flow margin.

Operating cash flow margin	2.7%)	3.4%
Financing cash flow margin	(1.7%)	(1.0%)
Net cash flow margin	**1.0%**	**2.4%**

Cash flow proof

Beginning cash from prior-period balance sheet	$154	$202
Plus operating cash flow	127	163
Plus financing cash flow	(79)	(47)
Must equal cash from current-period balance sheet	$202	$318

Durson had positive operating cash flow and used part of that to pay off debt and the remaining cash was added to cash on hand. Cash flow for the three-year period is strong.

The cash flow worksheet for Durson is on the following page.

Cash Flow Worksheet

Line		Note	20X2	20X3
1	Net profit (loss)	1	191	147
2	Change in current assets—excluding cash	2	22	31
3	Change in current liabilities—excluding bank and shareholder debt	3	(109)	(60)
4	Change in net fixed assets	4	25	40
5	Change in noncurrent assets	5	(2)	5
6	**Equals operating cash flow**	6	**127**	**163**
7	Operating cash flow margin	7	2.7%	3.4%
8	Change in bank/lease debt	8	(58)	(30)
9	Change in shareholder debt	9	-0-	-0-
10	Change in other long-term debt	10	-0-	-0-
11	Equity adjustment	11	(21)	(17)
12	**Equals financing cash flow**	12	**(79)**	**(47)**
13	Financing cash flow margin	13	(1.7%)	(1.0%)
14	**Net cash flow—line 6 + line 12**	14	**48**	**116**
15	Net cash flow margin	15	1.0%	2.4%
	Cash flow proof			
16	Prior-period cash from the balance sheet	16	154	202
17	+ net cash flow—Line 14	17	48	116
18	Equals current-period cash from the balance sheet	18	202	318

Notes:

1. Enter net profit or loss from the current-period income statement.
2. Always subtract the current-period from the prior-period to calculate this change.
3. Always subtract the prior-period from the current-period to calculate this change.
4. Always subtract the current-period from the prior-period to calculate this change.
5. Always subtract the current-period from the prior-period to calculate this change.
6. Operating cash flow equals the sum of lines 1–5.
7. Divide operating cash flow on line 6 by sales to calculate the operating cash flow margin (OpCFM).
8. Always subtract the prior-period from the current-period to calculate this change.
9. Always subtract the prior-period from the current-period to calculate this change.
10. Always subtract the prior-period from the current-period to calculate this change.
11. Subtract current-period net profit and prior-period equity from current-period equity to get the equity adjustment.
12. Financing cash flow equals the sum of lines 8–11.
13. Divide financing cash flow on line 12 by sales to calculate the financing cash flow margin (FinCFM).
14. Net cash flow is the sum of operating cash flow and financing cash flow, line 6 and line 12.
15. Divide net cash flow on line 14 by sales to calculate the net cash flow margin (NetCFM).
16. Cash from the prior-period balance sheet.
17. Net cash flow from line 14.
18. The sum of lines 16 and 17 that must equal cash on the current-period balance sheet.

OTHER TYPES OF CASH FLOW

There are two other types of cash flow with which you should be familiar. One is daily cash flow and the other is seasonal cash flow.

DAILY CASH FLOW
At the beginning of the day, you have a certain amount of cash. That is adjusted by such things as collection of accounts receivable, cash receipts from consumer moves, payment of expenses, etc. as follows:

Beginning cash
Plus:
> Accounts receivable collections
> Cash receipts
> Investment income

Minus:
> Accounts payable payments
> Loan/lease payments
> Payroll payments
> Other expenses payments

Equals ending cash

Cash receipts and disbursements are not difficult to project in the short term based upon historical experience. This type of forecasting is important to determine the amount and timing of payments when cash is tight. When creditors call to inquire about when they will receive payment, you can give them an answer that should be reasonably accurate.

If you have a cash flow problem in your business, you should forecast daily cash flow for a period of at least a month ahead to ensure you have sufficient cash flow on a daily basis.

SEASONAL CASH FLOW
Many businesses are seasonal and this can have a dramatic impact on cash flow since accounts receivable grow along with sales. This is illustrated by the following diagram.

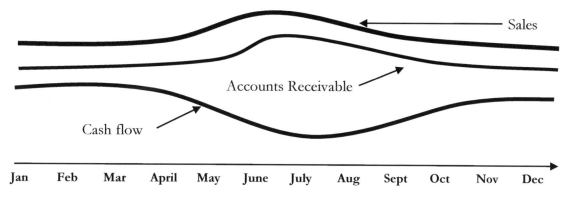

As accounts receivable goes *up*, cash flow goes *down*, causing a need for a seasonal bank line of credit unless the business has sufficient cash on hand to fund the shortfall. As accounts receivable run off cash flow is positive, allowing for the repayment of the line of credit.

You should have a zero balance on your line of credit at the end of the year. If you do not, it is because of one or more of the following reasons:

1.   Sales have grown at a high percentage in that year.
2.   Days sales outstanding (DSO) have increased beyond historical levels.
3.   Working capital is not sufficient.
4.   A combination of the above.

Correct this situation with good financial management and attention to the ratios outlined in this book so that you can pay off your line of credit by the end of the year.

DIVERSIFICATION

Note what happens in the diagram below if you are able to diversify and reduce the seasonality of your business. Cash flow does not go down but builds nicely throughout the year, as does sales. Since there are no losing months, the business is significantly more profitable and saves interest expense because there is little need for a line of credit.

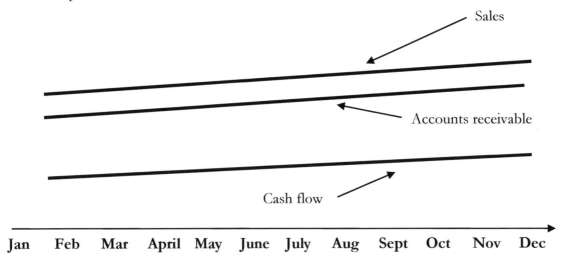

Build diversification into your long-term business strategy if possible, and avoid losing money several months a year.

STRATEGIES FOR MAXIMIZING CASH FLOW

Cash is king. The following are steps that you can take to maximize cash flow in your business.

1. Collect your accounts receivable on a timely basis. Get an aging of your accounts receivable every week, and have someone regularly call the oldest ones. No more than 5 to 10 percent of your total accounts receivable should be in the over-sixty-day category.
2. Invoice promptly. You cannot collect money until you've sent an invoice to the customer.
3. Diversify into non-seasonal lines of business if possible. This will reduce the seasonality of your business and help cash flow on a year-round basis.

4. Manage growth carefully. A high growth rate in sales causes growth in assets, which creates negative operating cash flow.
5. Borrow as long-term as possible. Payments are lower, and you can always pay the loan off sooner if justified by cash flow.
6. Never use short-term sources of cash (line of credit) to fund a long-term asset (equipment).
7. Maximize your net profit margin. Get as much bang for your sales buck as you can.
8. Minimize the purchase of fixed assets. Buy assets only when absolutely necessary. Rent in the short term, and/or lease assets with no down payment if possible.

Start thinking about cash flow in your business as much as you think about profits. Measure and then forecast the two types of cash flow as described in this chapter. Read this chapter again, and do the homework assignment at the end. Always remember that *cash is king*.

SUMMARY

The following is a summary of what we learned about the financial condition of Durson Distributors as a result of our analysis.

1. Liquidity is strong and getting better.
2. Safety is strong and getting better.
3. Overall, the balance sheet is strong and improving.
4. Profitability is marginal and declining.
5. Growth in sales is nonexistent and trending downward.
6. Return on equity is poor and getting worse, although this is commensurate with the low level of risk as indicated by the low debt-to-equity ratio.
7. Days sales outstanding are stable and at the industry average
8. Inventory days are trending slightly upward and are a little over the industry average.
9. Payable days are trending downward and are at the industry average.
10. The Z score is very good and getting better.
11. Operating cash flow is strong.
12. Financing cash flow is negative, indicating the repayment of debt.
13. Net cash flow is positive.

There is nothing difficult about this analysis and the above points are easy to see. It involves calculating twelve key relationships that allow you to determine liquidity, safety, profitability, operating performance, and cash flow. It's a fairly simple and quick exercise, and software is available on my website, www.leadtosucceed.biz, that does it for you automatically.

Study these ratios and reflect back on the phases of business and you can see that Durson Distributors is solidly in the plunder phase of business. The balance sheet and cash flow are strong, and debt is low. Sales growth is minimal but profits are consistent. Julian Durson has spent most of his life building a solid business with $5 million in sales and he is well-respected in the industry. He is the past president of his trade association, the downtown Rotary Club, and the Pleasant Hills Golf and Country Club, where he is currently a member of the board of trustees.

Dad may be pleased with the current situation, but Allen has a different opinion. He has seized on this analysis to renew his efforts to get dad to retire. The sales staff is ancient; profits are moribund; growth is nonexistent and the competition is eating their lunch. It will not be long, in his not-so-humble opinion, before they lose many of their major accounts to more aggressive competitors. It is easy to see that things are in bad straits, and he is at a loss to understand why dad cannot see this.

In desperation, he enlists the aid of his mom Sara. She is smart and well-educated but has never been involved in the business and does not understand a lot of what Allen is talking about. She has, however, been after Julian for several years to spend more time at their Florida condominium. She and Julian teamed up to win the over-sixty mixed doubles championship at the Breezy Palms Racket Club, and she wants another win this year. Allen's arguments play right into her desires for the future, and she is a willing ally in trying to convince Julian to retire and enjoy the fruits of his hard labor.

After several heated and emotional discussions, Julian finally agrees to head south with Sara and let Allen take over the business. He declined the opportunity to gift stock to Allen, but agreed that if things went well he would think about a plan to sell or gift some of the stock to him at some time in the future.

The following page is a summary of the ratios for Durson Distributors through 20X3. Study it, and observe how easy it is to spot strengths and weaknesses and determine appropriate solutions.

This business has done well historically, but cannot continue successfully on its present course because the competition will continually erode its customer base with more aggressive selling. It either needs dad to completely change his ways or it needs new and fresh leadership to restore sales growth. Fully understand what has happened and why, and pledge to calculate these ratios on a monthly basis in your business.

Durson Distributors
Ratio worksheet

	Formula	20X1	20X2	20X3	Industry Average
Liquidity					
Current ratio	current assets / current liabilities	2.38	2.97	3.89	2.60
Safety					
Debt to equity	total liabilities / equity	0.77	0.49	0.36	1.20
Profitability					
Gross profit margin	gross profit / sales	35.8%	35.2%	35.1%	36.2%
Operating profit margin	operating profit / sales	8.9%	4.4%	3.5%	6.0%
Net profit margin	net profit / sales	8.3%	4.0%	3.1%	5.0%
Operating Performance					
Return on equity (ROE)	net profit / equity	50.6%	18.3%	12.5%	29.8%
Days sales outstanding (DSO)	365 / accounts receivable turnover	41 days	46 days	39 days	36 days
Inventory days	365 / inventory turnover	49 days	53 days	58 days	56 days
Payable days	365 / accounts payable turnover	48 days	43 days	35 days	34 days
Z score	see below	8.1	8.7	10.0	5.0
Cash Flow					
Operating cash flow margin	operating cash flow / sales		2.7%	3.4%	NA
Financing cash flow margin	financing cash flow / sales		(1.7%)	(1.0%)	NA
Net cash flow margin	sum of cash flow margins		1.0%	2.4%	NA

The Z score is calculated as follows:

Current assets minus current liabilities
Total assets   x 6.56 = xx

Equity
Total assets   x 3.26 = xx

Profit before interest and taxes
Total assets   x 6.72 = xx

Equity
Total liabilities   x 1.05 = xx

Total   xxx

Grading	
0–1.0	Very bad
1.1–2.0	Poor
2.1–3.0	Fair
3.1–4.0	Good
4.1–5.0	Very good
5.0+	Excellent

SUMMARY

We have determined that looking at the *numbers* on your income statement and balance sheet does not tell you the whole story concerning your financial condition and may even be misleading. You need to look at *key relationships* in order to completely understand and determine your financial condition.

Think about what these ratios measure and why you are calculating them. Set goals and standards for your company, and then manage your business accordingly. When you master an understanding of these relationships, you will join an elite group of business owners who understand the financial dynamics of their businesses.

Financial management, taken step-by-step, is neither mysterious nor complicated. Problems, if any, are easy to spot, and solutions are also easy to see.

This chapter concludes our discussion of the twelve ratios that measure liquidity, safety, profitability, operating performance, and cash flow. Study them, and then go back and reread these chapters at least once a month. The only way you will fully learn and internalize these ratios is to use them regularly to help you manage a successful and profitable business.

Homework Assignment

Make two copies of the ratio worksheet at the end of this chapter, and fill in one for Durson Distributors, utilizing the income statements and balance sheets in prior chapters. This will help you understand where all of the numbers have come from.

Use the second copy to calculate the ratios for your business. Do not delegate this homework assignment to your CFO or accounting manager. Do it yourself. This exercise will do more to enable you to understand the financial ratios and condition of your business than anything else you might do. Ask your banker or local librarian for a copy of the Risk Management Association (RMA) ratio averages for your industry, and put those on the worksheet in place of the averages for Durson Distributors. If you have trouble locating the averages for your industry e-mail me at dave@leadtosucceed.biz and I will send them to you if they exist.

Make two copies of the cash flow worksheet at the end of this chapter, and fill in one for Durson Distributors. This will help you understand the principles of cash flow and how to measure it.

Use the second copy to calculate cash flow for your business. Do not delegate this assignment to your CFO. Get four years of your year-end financial statements, and fill in the three columns on the form. By the time you finish this exercise, you will have a good grasp on cash flow in your business.

The next chapter will discuss Durson Distributors—the next generation. Keep on paddling!

Financial Ratio Worksheet

	Formula	year____	year____	year____	Industry Average
Liquidity					
Current ratio	current assets / current liabilities				
Safety					
Debt to equity	total liabilities / equity				
Profitability					
Gross profit margin	gross profit / sales				
Operating profit margin	operating profit / sales				
Net profit margin	net profit / sales				
Operating Performance					
Return on equity (ROE)	net profit / equity				
Days sales outstanding (DSO)	365 / accounts receivable turnover				
Inventory days	365 / inventory turnover				
Payable days	365 / accounts payable turnover				
Z score	see below				5.0
Cash Flow					
Operating cash flow margin	operating cash flow / sales				NA
Financing cash flow margin	financing cash flow / sales				NA
Net cash flow margin	sum of cash flow margins				NA

The Z score is calculated as follows:

Current assets minus current liabilities / Total assets   x 6.56 = xx

Equity / Total assets   x 3.26 = xx

Profit before interest and taxes / Total assets   x 6.72 = xx

Equity / Total liabilities   x 1.05 = xx

Total   xxx

Grading	
0–1.0	Very bad
1.1–2.0	Poor
2.1–3.0	Fair
3.1–4.0	Good
4.1–5.0	Very good
5.0+	Excellent

Cash Flow Worksheet

Line		Note	Year_____	Year_____	Year_____
1	Net profit (loss)	1			
2	Change in current assets—excluding cash	2			
3	Change in current liabilities—excluding bank and shareholder debt	3			
4	Change in net fixed assets	4			
5	Change in noncurrent assets	5			
6	**Equals operating cash flow**	6			
7	**Operating cash flow margin**	7			
8	Change in bank/lease debt	8			
9	Change in shareholder debt	9			
10	Change in other long-term debt	10			
11	Equity adjustment	11			
12	**Equals financing cash flow**	12			
13	**Financing cash flow margin**	13			
14	**Net cash flow—line 6 + line 12**	14			
15	**Net cash flow margin**	15			
	Cash flow proof				
16	Prior-period cash from the balance sheet	16			
17	+ net cash flow—Line 14	17			
18	Equals current-period cash from the balance sheet	18			

Notes:
1. Enter net profit or loss from the current-period income statement.
2. Always subtract the current-period from the prior-period to calculate this change.
3. Always subtract the prior-period from the current-period to calculate this change.
4. Always subtract the current-period from the prior-period to calculate this change.
5. Always subtract the current-period from the prior-period to calculate this change.
6. Operating cash flow equals the sum of lines 1–5.
7. Divide operating cash flow on line 6 by sales to calculate the operating cash flow margin (OpCFM).
8. Always subtract the prior-period from the current-period to calculate this change.
9. Always subtract the prior-period from the current-period to calculate this change.
10. Always subtract the prior-period from the current-period to calculate this change.
11. Subtract current-period net profit and prior-period equity from current-period equity to get the equity adjustment.
12. Financing cash flow equals the sum of lines 8–11.
13. Divide financing cash flow on line 12 by sales to calculate the financing cash flow margin (FinCFM).
14. Net cash flow is the sum of operating cash flow and financing cash flow, line 6 and line 12.
15. Divide net cash flow on line 14 by sales to calculate the net cash flow margin (NetCFM).
16. Cash from the prior-period balance sheet.
17. Net cash flow from line 14.
18. The sum of lines 16 and 17 that must equal cash on the current-period balance sheet.

CHAPTER NINE: DURSON DISTRIBUTORS– THE NEXT GENERATION

Allen sat contentedly in his dad's chair and proudly surveyed his new domain. It did not take him long to move into his dad's office which, with conference table and private bath, was nearly twice the size of his. A trophy wall contained the many awards he had won as a top salesman. Pictures of his lovely wife, Debbie, and twin girls, Elizabeth and Caroline, adorned his credenza. Dad's files had been moved to Allen's old office so that he would have a place to sit on the hopefully rare times that he would visit. It was exhilarating to finally be in charge, and he was almost dizzy with excitement.

Allen arranged for the sales staff to retire, hired a new VP of sales, and three new salespeople. He hired a firm to update the marketing brochures and he assigned territories and set aggressive sales goals for the salespeople.

He had his eye on two promising locations in neighboring states and began immediately to search out potential locations for new branches of the company. He opened the first new branch in late 20X4 and the second one a year later. He was determined that Durson Distributors would not be left behind in the economic expansion that the industry was currently experiencing.

His work and planning were rewarded by a significant growth in sales, which averaged nearly 40 percent per year. By the end of 20X6 sales were over $13 million, more than twice the best year the company had ever had. He took the entire sales staff and their families on a five-day cruise to the Bahamas as a reward for their hard work. Allen was pleased with himself, and morale in the company was off the charts.

His sales successes were not lost on several vendors who rewarded him with an all-expense-paid trip to Disney World in 20X5 and 20X6.

Amid all of this celebrating, things were not quite so rosy at the bank. Allen had financed this growth primarily with bank debt, and the once solid balance sheets did not have quite the rosy glow that they used to have. Conversations with the banker became increasingly strained and this was baffling to Allen. Both sales and operating profit had doubled in a short three year time period, and he thought that everyone should be singing his praises. Instead, the banker was making noises about restricting loans to the company going forward.

Dad was not too pleased either when Allen asked him to loan the company money in 20X5 and 20X6. He was lulled into acceptance by the glowing reports he received from Allen, but he could not understand why he had to put money into the company if things were going so well.

Sales were up, operating profit was up, but cash flow was, unfortunately, not up.
The following are the balance sheets for the period 20X1 to 20X6.

Durson Distributors
Balance sheet (000)

	Julian Years			Allen Years		
	20X1	20X2	20X3	20X4	20X5	20X6
Cash	$154	$202	$318	108	$90	$104
Trade accounts receivable	601	595	510	845	1,325	1,999
Inventory	463	445	497	978	1,560	2,601
Other current assets	37	39	41	55	84	101
Current assets	$1,255	$1,281	$1,366	$1,986	$3,059	$4,805
Gross fixed assets	862	887	895	1,301	1,789	2,100
Accumulated depreciation	(602)	(652)	(700)	(768)	(888)	(1,068)
Net fixed assets	260	235	195	533	901	1,032
Other assets	35	37	32	44	52	55
Total assets	$1,550	$1,553	$1,593	$2,563	$4,012	$5,892
Line of credit-bank	-0-	-0-	-0-	194	773	1,436
Trade accounts payable	451	359	300	560	888	1,619
Accrued expenses	38	21	20	45	66	97
Current portion long-term bank debt	39	52	31	55	102	118
Current liabilities	$528	$432	$351	$854	$1,829	$3,270
Long-term bank debt	147	76	67	423	683	947
Shareholder debt	-0-	-0-	-0-	-0-	100	150
Total liabilities	$675	$508	$418	$1,277	$2,612	$4,367
Capital stock	75	75	75	75	75	75
Retained earnings	800	970	1,100	1,211	1,325	1,450
Equity	$875	$1,045	1,175	$1,286	$1,400	$1,525
Total liabilities and equity	$1,550	$1,553	$1,593	$2,563	$4,012	$5,892

Allen looked at these balance sheets and saw that total assets and equity were both up and concluded that things were good. For the life of him he could not understand what the banker's problem was, and he seriously considered looking around for another bank that would be more appreciative of the progress that he has made as president of the company.

Allen's observations are interesting, but let's take a look at the ratios that measure liquidity and safety and see how the balance sheets are actually performing.

LIQUIDITY—SECOND GENERATION

The following are the current ratios for Durson for the periods 20X1 through 20X6:

	Julian			Allen			Industry
	20X1	20X2	20X3	20X4	20X5	20X6	Average
Current ratio	2.38	2.97	3.89	2.23	1.67	1.47	2.60

Liquidity has declined dramatically from 20X3 to 20X6 and is now substantially less than the industry average. A current ratio of 1.47 means that the company has $1.47 in current assets to pay $1.00 of current liabilities, or $.47 in working capital, down from $2.89 in 20X3.

SAFETY—SECOND GENERATION

	Julian			Allen			Industry
	20X1	20X2	20X3	20X4	20X5	20X6	Average
Debt-to-equity	0.77	0.49	0.36	0.99	1.87	2.86	1.10

A quick look is enough to see why the banker is alarmed. Safety has deteriorated badly since 20X1, and the debt-to-equity ratio is now well over twice the industry average. A debt-to-equity ratio of 2.86 means that the company has $2.86 in liabilities for every $1.00 of equity. In other words, the creditors have almost three times more invested in the business than the owner does. The higher the debt-to-equity ratio, the less safe is the business.

Assets are up and equity is up. The *numbers* tell us that the balance sheets are good and getting better, but the *ratios* tell us that safety is bad and getting worse.

This is an example of the value of routinely calculating your financial ratios. Your accounting system provides you with financial statements (the numbers), but few accounting systems provide a complete ratio analysis, if any at all.

PROFITABILITY—SECOND GENERATION

The company is not doing well as far as the balance sheets are concerned, but let's take a look at how the income statements are doing.

The income statements for the years 20X1—20X6 are on the following page.

Durson Distributors
Income statement (000)

	Julian Years			Allen Years		
	20X1	20X2	20X3	20X4	20X5	20X6
Sales	**$5,368**	**$4,750**	**$4,805**	**$6,555**	**$9,177**	**$13,100**
Cost of goods sold	3,446	3,078	3,118	4,274	6,048	8,725
Gross profit	**$1,922**	**$1,672**	**$1,687**	**$2,281**	**$3,129**	**$4,375**
Advertising	72	70	65	89	125	180
Bad debts	51	45	40	64	81	95
Depreciation	49	50	48	70	95	126
Equipment leases	17	16	18	30	61	88
Insurance	71	80	92	110	150	201
Legal and accounting	13	15	17	25	31	33
Miscellaneous	39	27	34	35	46	81
Office expenses	29	33	32	48	55	71
Payroll tax and benefits	146	148	153	200	281	412
Rent	100	100	100	187	210	325
Repairs and maintenance	31	29	30	22	36	31
Salaries	520	528	560	735	1,039	1,480
Sales commissions	145	144	136	172	236	393
Business tax and license	27	25	31	35	60	72
Telephone and utilities	38	41	42	48	47	52
Travel and entertainment	21	24	33	65	95	147
Vehicle expenses	73	88	90	109	152	201
Total overhead expenses	1,442	1,463	1,521	2,044	2,800	3,988
Operating profit	**$480**	**$209**	**$166**	**$237**	**$329**	**$387**
Other income	15	18	20	19	21	28
Other expenses	(39)	(27)	(32)	(40)	(55)	(51)
Interest expense	(13)	(9)	(7)	(47)	(109)	(175)
Net profit	**$443**	**$191**	**$147**	**$169**	**$186**	**$189**

Allen looks at these numbers and feels more than vindicated. He set out to increase sales, and that is exactly what he has done. All of his hard work over the last three years has paid off handsomely, and he is already scouting out another location for expansion in 20X7 or 20X8.

Of course, as we have already learned, the *relationships* (financial ratios) may tell a different story than the *numbers*. The following are the profitability ratios for the last six years:

	Julian			Allen			Industry
	20X1	20X2	20X3	20X4	20X5	20X6	Average
Gross profit margin	35.8%	35.2%	35.1%	34.8%	34.1%	33.4%	36.2%
Oper. profit margin	8.9%	4.4%	3.5%	3.6%	3.6%	3.0%	6.0%
Net profit margin	8.3%	4.0%	3.1%	2.6%	2.0%	1.4%	5.0%

Sales have grown dramatically, and operating profit in 20X6 is over twice what it was in 20X3 in dollar amount, but the *relationships* reflect that profitability is virtually in free-fall. The 1.4 percent net profit margin in 20X6 is the lowest that the company has ever experienced since Julian founded it thirty-five years ago.

The cause of this is not too difficult to determine. The gross profit margin has declined from 35.8 percent to 33.4 percent and is significantly below the industry average. This drop in the gross profit margin has caused a dramatic reduction in the net profit margin. In addition, interest expense has risen dramatically since bank debt was largely used to finance the negative operating cash flow.

If the company could have maintained the gross profit margin of 35.8 percent that was experienced in 20X1, the net profit would have been 2.4 percent larger in 20X6. That would have produced a net profit of $503, as follows:

Sales	$13,100	100.0%
Gross profit margin	4,690	35.8%%
Less overhead expenses	(3,988)	(30.4%)
Operating profit	702	5.4%
Less other income & expenses	(198)	(1.5%)
Equals net profit	$504	3.9%

An increase in the gross profit margin of 2.4 percent produces an increase in net profit of 166 percent ($189 to $503)! You can see why constant monitoring of the gross profit margin is so important. Every dollar increase at that level drops right to the bottom line. An increase of even 0.1 percent would result in a $13k increase in net profit. Make sure to calculate this ratio for your business and investigate the cause of a drop of even 0.1 percent.

OPERATING PERFORMANCE—SECOND GENERATION

So far we have declining liquidity, safety, and profitability as a result of calculating five key ratios, and these problems were not at all difficult to spot. Now let's take a look at the operating performance ratios under Allen's leadership.

	Julian			Allen			Industry Average
	20X1	**20X2**	**20X3**	**20X4**	**20X5**	**20X6**	
Return on equity	50.7%	18.3%	12.5%	13.1%	13.3%	12.4%	29.8%
Days sales outstanding	41	46	39	47	53	56	36
Inventory days	49	53	58	84	94	109	56
Payable days	48	43	35	48	54	68	34
Z score	8.1	8.7	10.0	6.1	4.1	3.3	5.0

Return on equity (reward) has continued to decline and is currently less than half of the industry average. The really bad news is that at the same time the debt-to-equity ratio has gone up dramatically. This means that the company has more risk and less reward, exactly the opposite of what you want to happen.

Accounts receivable and inventory have ballooned up in the last three years, and this has sucked up precious cash (as assets go *up*, cash goes *down*). This is a direct result of opening two new branches and not paying attention to these key ratios.

Accounts payable days have doubled, and this is a result of the drop in liquidity and the resulting inability to pay bills when they are due. If you have customers that are late in paying you, the chances are very likely this is the reason why. The working capital is not sufficient.

The Z score has declined precipitously, indicating that the overall financial health of the company has deteriorated.

CASH FLOW—SECOND GENERATION

By now you can begin to imagine that cash flow is probably disastrous. Sales have gone up dramatically, causing assets to go up dramatically, and causing cash flow to go down dramatically. A lot of drama and a lot of stress. The lack of positive operating cash flow has been made up by a combination of a reduction in the amount of cash on hand and an increase in financing cash flow.

OPERATING CASH FLOW

The following is the operating cash flow for the six-year period.

	Julian		Allen			Industry Average
	20X2	**20X3**	**20X4**	**20X5**	**20X6**	
Operating cash flow	127	163	(726)	(932)	(915)	NA
OpCF Margin	2.7%	3.4%	(11.1%)	(10.2%)	(7.0%)	NA

Good old dad may have been conservative and unwilling to take any risks, but he *was* able to generate positive operating cash flow. In the last three years of his stewardship, the company made $855 in operating profit and had positive operating cash flow of $290 (127+163). Perhaps this did not set the world on fire, but it was not so bad either.

In the period since Allen has taken over, the company made $953 in operating profit and had negative operating cash flow of $2,573 (726+932+915)—fairly good profits but terrible cash flow!

FINANCING CASH FLOW

The following is the financing cash flow for the six year period:

| | Julian | | Allen | | | Industry |
	20X2	20X3	20X4	20X5	20X6	Average
Financing cash flow	(79)	(47)	517	914	929	NA
FinCF Margin	(1.7%)	(1.0%)	7.9%	10.0%	7.1%	NA

Dad paid off $126 in debt (79+47), and son managed to get the company $2,360 deeper in debt when he took over in 20X4 (517+914+929). As you can imagine, both the banker and dad were not at all pleased about this, and both demanded corrective action be taken. Take note that the increase in debt was *not* the problem, it was the increase in the debt-to-equity ratio with the corresponding drop in safety that was the source of the trouble. Put yourself in the shoes of the banker and you can see why he is not happy.

The following is the cash flow for Durson Distributors reflecting operating cash flow and financing cash flow for the last six years.

Cash Flow Worksheet

Line		Julian Years		Allen Years		
		20X2	20X3	20X4	20X5	20X6
1	Net profit (loss)	191	147	169	186	189
2	Change in current assets—excluding cash	22	31	(830)	(1,091)	(1,732)
3	Change in current liabilities—excluding bank and shareholder debt	(109)	(60)	315	319	762
4	Change in net fixed assets	25	40	(338)	(368)	(131)
5	Change in noncurrent assets	(2)	5	(12)	(8)	(3)
6	**Equals operating cash flow**	**127**	**163**	**(696)**	**(962)**	**(915)**
7	Operating cash flow margin	2.7%	3.4%	(11.1%)	(10.2%)	(7.0%)
8	Change in bank/lease debt	(58)	(30)	574	886	943
9	Change in shareholder debt	-0-	-0-	-0-	100	50
10	Change in other long-term debt	-0-	-0-	-0-	-0-	-0-
11	Equity adjustment	(21)	(17)	(58)	(72)	(64)
12	**Equals financing cash flow**	**(79)**	**(47)**	**516**	**914**	**929**
13	**Financing cash flow margin**	**(1.7%)**	**(1.0%)**	**7.9%**	**10.0%**	**7.1%**
14	**Net cash flow—line 6 + line 12**	**48**	**116**	**(210)**	**(18)**	**14**
15	**Net cash flow margin**	**1.0%**	**2.4%**	**(3.2%)**	**(0.2%)**	**0.1%**
	Cash flow proof					
16	Prior-period cash from the balance sheet	154	202	318	108	90
17	+ net cash flow—Line 14	48	116	(210)	(18)	14
18	Equals current-period cash from the balance sheet	202	318	108	90	104

Operating cash flow, line 6, has gone from positive in the Julian years to dramatically negative in the Allen years. This was caused by the significant increase in sales which caused an increase in assets which caused a decrease in operating cash flow. As assets go *up*, cash flow goes *down*. Picture in your mind one or two more years of this kind of "success" for Durson Distributors. The bank will shut off loans and demand repayment and the company may have to go out of business. It's called *growing broke*.

Financing cash flow, line 12, has gone from negative in the Julian years (debt was reduced), to positive in the Allen years (debt was increased). Allen has used a combination of bank, trade, and shareholder debt to fund the growth in the company. He felt justified in doing this because the company was so "successful" under his leadership.

Growth is good, but it needs to be managed carefully. More on this later in this chapter.

The following are the financial and cash flow ratios for Durson Distributors for the Julian and Allen years.

	Julian years			Allen years			Industry Average
	20X1	20X2	20X3	20X4	20X5	20X6	
Liquidity							
Current ratio	2.38	2.97	3.89	2.33	1.67	1.47	2.60
Safety							
Debt-to-equity	0.77	0.49	0.36	0.99	1.87	2.86	1.20
Profitability							
Gross profit margin	35.8%	35.2%	35.1%	34.8%	34.1%	33.4%	36.2%
Operating profit margin	8.9%	4.4%	3.5%	3.6%	3.6%	3.0%	6.0%
Net profit margin	8.3%	4.0%	3.1%	2.6%	2.0%	1.4%	5.0%
Operating Performance							
Return on equity (ROE)	50.7%	18.3%	12.5%	13.1%	13.3%	12.4%	29.8%
Days sales outstanding (DSO)	41 days	46 days	39 days	47 days	53 days	56 days	36 days
Inventory days	49 days	53 days	58 days	84 days	94 days	109 days	56 days
Payable days	48 days	43 days	35days	48 days	54 days	68 days	34 days
Z score	8.1	8.7	10.0	6.1	4.1	3.3	5.0
Cash Flow							
Operating cash flow margin		2.7%	3.4%	(11.1)	(10.2%)	(7.0%)	NA
Financing cash flow margin		(1.7%)	(1.0%)	7.9%	10.0%	7.1%	NA
Net cash flow margin		1.0%	2.4%	(3.2%)	(0.2%)	0.1%	NA

The problems in 20X6 are easy to spot:
1. Liquidity is poor and getting worse.
2. Safety is terrible and getting worse.
3. Profitability is terrible and getting worse.
4. Return on equity is terrible and not commensurate with the risk as reflected by the increased debt-to-equity ratio.
5. Days sales outstanding are terrible and getting worse.
6. Inventory days are terrible and getting worse.
7. Payable days are terrible and getting worse.
8. The Z score is OK in 20X6, but declining rapidly.
9. Operating cash flow is terrible.
10. Aside from a loan to the company of $150k by Julian and an increase in trade payables, the bank has funded all of the negative operating cash flow. Thus the debt-to-equity ratio has gone up and the safety of the company has deteriorated.

At the insistence of the banker, Julian flew up from Florida, and they met with Allen in the bank's conference room. The banker said that he was alarmed at the deterioration in the safety of the company and announced that he was not going to provide any additional loans and demanded that existing loans be paid down so that the debt-to-equity ratio would be no higher than 2.00.

Allen was offended and defensive, and Julian was apoplectic. His name (not Allen's) was on the personal guarantees at the bank, and he could easily visualize his nest egg evaporating. He was in a vicious mood, and it was fortunate that no weapon was available or he might have done something rash. He could not imagine how he was going to explain to Sara that their comfortable lifestyle was doomed if this situation could not be salvaged.

The banker was fearful about his loan and upset that the long-time relationship with his friend Julian was deteriorating. Dad was fearful and upset about the deteriorating state of the business and his personal financial situation. Allen was upset and angry about being criticized for what he believed to be spectacular performance.

Before blows could be exchanged, the banker managed to get everyone calmed down enough to focus on finding solutions to the current situation.

After a lot of discussion, they decided to do the following things:

1. Allen would cease all efforts to grow sales, work on generating positive operating cash flow, and abandon any plans to open another branch.
2. A temporary person would be hired immediately to work on collecting past-due accounts receivable with the goal of reducing days sales outstanding to no more than forty days by the end of March.
3. Allen would carefully analyze the inventory and reduce inventory days to no more than forty-five by the end of February. Slower moving items would be moved at a discount if necessary.
4. There would be an immediate freeze on hiring and raises until further notice.
5. Allen would come up with a plan for laying off staff if it became necessary to do so.
6. Cash generated from the reduction in the above-mentioned assets (as assets go *down* cash goes *up*) would go first to reduce bank debt and then to reduce accounts payable, if any was available. No payment would be made on the loan of $150 to Julian without permission from the bank in writing.

Allen was skeptical that this could be accomplished in such a short time without seriously reducing prices, but he promised to do his best.

You can calculate how much cash the above steps would generate as follows.

1. Determine sales per day by dividing sales by 365.

    $13,100 ÷ 365 = $36

2. Multiply sales per day by the planned reduction in days sales outstanding of 16.

   $36 x 16 = $576

   $576 is the amount of cash that will be generated by the reduction in accounts receivable. As assets go *down*, cash flow goes *up*.

3. Determine inventory per day by dividing cost of goods sold by 365.

   $8,725 ÷ 365 = $24

4. Multiply inventory per day by the planned reduction in inventory days of 64 days.

   $24 x 64 = $1,536

   $1,536 is the amount of cash that will be generated by the reduction in inventory. As assets go *down*, cash flow goes *up*.

These two efforts were projected to generate $2,112 in positive operating cash flow which would be used to reduce bank debt. The banker agreed to continue to finance the operations on a day by day basis, with the stipulation that the line of credit would be paid off by no later than the end of March. This would take $1,436, leaving $676 that could be paid to past due trade creditors (who were no longer offering free trips to Disney World).

Allen didn't like any of this, but when faced with complying with this plan *or else*, he finally agreed. He recognized this as a near-death experience and he wanted to placate dad and keep his job.

This plan took a little longer than expected, as plans often do, but Julian, who willingly put golf on the back burner, and Allen, worked together and were able to get Durson Distributors back on a firm footing by the end of 150 days. The banker was keenly interested in the process and carefully monitored the progress in reducing bank debt.

Julian and Allen both finally understood that this crisis did not need to happen in the first place. If *anyone* at Durson Distributors had been calculating these ratios on a regular basis, the problems would have been spotted well in advance and allowed for corrective action. Of course there was no one at Durson Distributors who would have understood what the ratios meant if they had been calculated. They believed that more sales and profits are good, no matter what. Obviously they needed a copy of this book!

I urge you to calculate these twelve ratios on a monthly basis. How long does this take—15 minutes? Of course it won't do any good if no one knows what the ratios mean or why they are important. Keep this book handy on your credenza and read the chapters describing financial ratios every month. Keep paddling in these waters until you know instinctively and intuitively where you are and where you are going. Use it or lose it. *What gets measured gets managed, and what gets managed gets fixed.*

This analysis process is not complicated. Be sure to visit www.leadtosucceed.biz and download the software that will assist you in making these calculations.

SUMMARY

Julian Durson founded a company at the age of thirty-four, with a little help from mom and dad, and worked hard over the years to build it into a sound and profitable company. He was a person who cared about his employees, his family, and the community and he gave back to all of them. At age sixty-nine he was pleased with how it had turned out. He had a lovely home in a nice neighborhood, a three-bedroom condo in Florida, and a comfortable thirty-two foot express cruiser that performed well in the gulf waters.

At the end of 20X3, when Julian retired, things may not have been absolutely perfect but the glass was half full for sure. The company was safe, liquid, profitable, and had good cash flow. It was solidly in the plunder phase of business and Julian could not find anything to be unhappy about. Life was good, and he was especially pleased that his son Allen had decided to join the company as the successful director of sales.

Julian and Allen had a great relationship, both on and off the job, but clashes on growth strategies were inevitable. Dad was comfortable and son was frustrated. He wanted dad to grow the business. Dad always responded by saying "OK, that's something we could consider," but then he did absolutely nothing. This was not Allen's idea of progress.

When Allen, in desperation, enlisted mom's help in getting dad out of the way, the momentum began to shift. Julian loved Sara and wanted her to be happy, and, truth be told, he wouldn't mind playing a little more golf and tennis and spending more time on the water. He had confidence in his son, who he often boasted "could sell ice cubes to igloo dwellers," so he went south with his bride to enjoy the Florida sun. Allen was unleashed to grow the company, and the rest is history.

All of the pain that came later could have been avoided by calculating twelve simple ratios on a regular basis, but that was not going to happen. Allen was a salesperson, not a finance person, and he neither respected nor particularly enjoyed being around numbers people. They tended to be nerdy, green eyeshade introverts whose apparent mission in life was to harass normal people and keep them from making any progress. It seemed like they were negative by nature, and spoke in a language that was both difficult to understand and irritating.

Allen knew what needed to be done and how to do it and entered a new blunder/renewal phase of business with a vengeance. Sales skyrocketed, and cash flow plummeted. Interested parties like the banker and trade creditors started to get less and less cordial, just when everyone should have proclaimed him business man of the year. All of this culminated in a very emotional meeting in the bank's conference room.

I hope you see how that meeting could have been avoided. It is easy to spot problems by regularly calculating a few ratios. You do not need to become a certified financial analyst to do this. You just need to know twelve key relationships and what they mean. Excel software is available for free downloading at www.leadtosucceed.biz that will do all the calculating for you. Get it and use it. Avoid a confrontational meeting in your bank's conference room!

Allen grew the company very quickly, and got into financial difficulty. The next chapter will discuss growth management. Keep on paddling!

CHAPTER TEN: STRATEGIES FOR MANAGING GROWTH

Allen correctly recognized that Durson Distributors was in the plunder phase of business in 20X3 and needed to enter into a new phase of renewed growth. He was successful but he violated the basic principle that no one can grow as fast as they want. All firms are constrained by their available equity (capital), even public firms. Allen is sales-driven and believes that if a little sales growth is good, more is better. This may seem true on the surface, but there are financial limits to growth, and it needs to be carefully managed.

FINANCIAL DYNAMICS OF GROWTH

Growth in sales causes an increase in assets. If sales double, accounts receivable are likely to double. Inventory will double, and additional equipment will have to be purchased. The cash needed for this increase in assets must come from one or more of the following sources:

1. Net profit
2. New trade debt
3. New bank debt
4. Shareholder loan or equity investment
5. Existing cash on hand

If there is sufficient operating cash flow to fund needed assets, the business is financing itself on an *internal* basis. Unfortunately, if the rate of growth is significant, operating cash flow is rarely enough to fund all of the new assets required, so funding has to come from either new debt or addition to equity. As debt increases, the debt-to-equity ratio (and therefore risk) usually increases. Lines of credit become strained; payments to trade creditors are delayed; and eventually lawyers get into the act. Bankruptcy is just around the corner. It is called *growing broke*, and it happens even though sales and profits are strong.

The amount of assets caused by the increase in sales depends upon the rate of growth in Sales. This is illustrated by the following diagram.

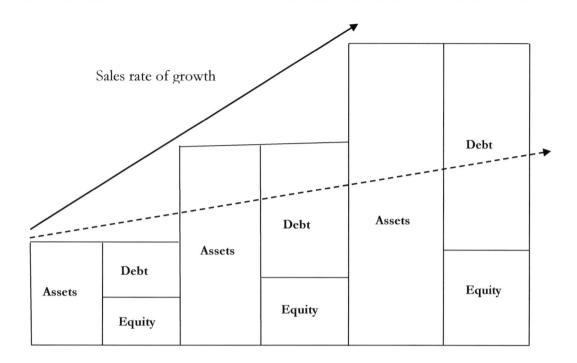

As you can see, growth in sales causes a growth in assets. Equity grows by the amount of the net profit (less distributions to shareholders), but net profit is usually not enough to fund all of the assets that are required.

In the above diagram, debt is growing at a faster rate than equity. This causes the debt-to-equity ratio to increase and the safety of the business to decrease, as described in chapter five. In other words, when debt is used to fund the growth in assets as the business experiences high growth in sales and net profit, the debt-to-equity ratio increases, and the company becomes more risky or less safe. The bank does not like this and it is difficult for the sales-oriented business owner to understand why not. Everything is great, so what is the problem?

High growth in sales, if carried to an extreme, can literally grow the company into bankruptcy, and negative operating cash flow is the reason. This is why your banker may ask you to reduce your rate of growth, even though increasing sales is your primary objective. Reducing the rate of growth in sales and net profit does not make intuitive sense and may not be what you want to do, but from a cash flow standpoint, growth must be carefully managed.

Note what happens when the rate of growth is reduced, as reflected by the dashed line. The relationship between debt and equity, which measures safety, is now fairly constant. The company is growing, but the debt-to-equity ratio is not growing, and the company is on a sound footing from a safety standpoint.

The financial truth is that no company can grow as fast as it wants to grow. All companies are limited by the amount of capital (equity) that they have and must be aware of the financial dynamics of growth and measure and track financial ratios regularly. Cash flow analysis is a vital aspect of this process, since negative operating cash flow, caused by a significant increase in assets is the problem.

PRINCIPLES FOR MAXIMIZING GROWTH

Growth of your business is good, but like most other things too much growth can be bad. In order to grow as fast as possible, you must employ three key strategies:

MINIMIZE YOUR ASSETS

A high turnover of inventory and accounts receivable (low inventory days and days sales outstanding ratios) will have the effect of minimizing the assets required. The purchase of fixed assets should also be minimized. The cash down payment required takes precious cash that is needed elsewhere in the business. Leasing or even renting of fixed assets should be given strong consideration, even if it is a little more expensive. If fixed assets are purchased, you should try to finance them over as long a period as possible in order to minimize the loan payments. This will minimize cash outflow and increase your ability to grow.

MAXIMIZE NET PROFIT MARGIN

Note that this does not say maximize *net profit*. It is important to get the highest margins possible at both the gross profit and net profit levels. High profit margins will increase the growth rate that is possible.

MAXIMIZE EQUITY

Every dime of earnings should be reinvested in the business. Resist the temptation to take out bonuses when the business starts to make a lot of money. Keep money in the business in order to have sufficient equity to fund the growth.

MANAGING GROWTH SUMMARY

Growth is desirable and even necessary, but it needs to be carefully managed. If you find yourself with the opportunity for high growth, make sure you understand the cash flow dynamics of your business. Lay out a financial plan, as discussed in chapters eleven through thirteen, and make sure that you adhere to the principles outlined in chapter eighteen in your dealings with the bank. You do not want to "grow broke."

The next chapter will discuss an introduction to planning, something that Durson Distributors desperately needs at this point. Keep on paddling!

CHAPTER ELEVEN: INTRODUCTION TO PLANNING

"If you don't know where you are going, you may wind up somewhere else."
"Fail to plan, plan to fail."

You pick the cliché, they are all applicable. Operating a business without a plan is like navigating without a compass—you never know where you might end up.

Most business owners resist planning. They tend to be action oriented, and the task immediately before them is what gets their attention.

REASONS FOR LACK OF PLANNING

LACK OF KNOWLEDGE
Learning how, what, and when to plan takes a fair amount of effort, and you may not know how to start. This book describes in detail how to generate a strategic and financial plan for your business.

LACK OF TIME
When I ask business owners why they don't plan, they frequently answer, "I don't have time for that. I am already working ten to twelve hours a day, six or seven days a week, struggling to be successful in this business. When am I supposed to find time to plan?"

Developing a business plan, especially the first time, *is* hard work. However, in the long run, planning doesn't *take* time, it *saves* time. Instead of answering the same questions over and over, you answer them once. With a plan you become *proactive* instead of *reactive*. You can measure your actual performance versus your plan and take action when necessary. Everything is more orderly and efficient, and you have more time to devote to your day-to-day activities.

FEAR
Fear of the unknown. Fear of being held accountable. Fear of not making your plan.

When you put a plan down on paper, others can see it. They will know if you don't achieve it. They may be critical of your performance. Who needs this? It's better and less stressful not to commit yourself in the first place.

On the other hand, without a written plan, your employees and leadership team will not know what it is you are trying to accomplish, and they will have no way of knowing whether they are succeeding or not. They want to do well and work for a successful business. They want to help you accomplish your goals, but without a plan they do not know what they are. Establishing a written plan will enhance your communications with them and will insure that everyone is on the same page, helping to achieve common goals.

UNCERTAINTY

The business climate has changed a lot in the past few years, and it promises to change even more in the future. With the uncertainty that such changes bring, why bother to put together a plan? It is just going to be obsolete soon anyway.

Facing an uncertain future is a major reason to establish goals and objectives and give careful thought to the establishment of a business plan. This will better prepare you to take advantage of opportunities and minimize the potential threats to your business.

RESULTS OF NOT PLANNING

The lack of planning is often the cause of either serious problems or outright failure. Poor management and planning is estimated to account for over 90 percent of business failures, rather than the state of the economy or the industry.

Learn how to develop a business plan, and invest time in this process. Don't use one of the above excuses as a reason not to plan.

STRATEGIC PLANNING

Effective business planning starts with a look at the big picture—the basic strategies the company should employ in the next few years. Failure to devote proper attention to this aspect of planning is akin to drifting in a boat down an unexplored river. All your effort is devoted to the task at hand, steering the boat away from the riverbanks and dangerous rocks so that it won't become damaged or stranded.

You don't give the low rumbling sound, barely perceptible in the distance, much thought. Things are going pretty well, and you are so busy guiding the boat away from trouble that you don't really have time to think about anything else. *Maybe that rumbling will go away.*

However, the rumbling gets progressively louder. Inevitably, you, the boat, and everyone in it are flung over an unseen and unplanned for (but nevertheless fatal) waterfall, landing on the rocks below.

Of course, the waterfall was avoidable. The increased rumblings gave ample warning that it was there, but everyone in the boat was busy with the tasks at hand and were not paying attention to anything else.

Kodak is a great example of a firm that ignored future indications of what the industry might look like. It stuck with film and ultimately declared bankruptcy. This happened even though they invented a digital camera, which they shelved because they saw it as a threat to their film business. Learn from others. Ignore that rumbling noise at your peril.

Elevating your sights occasionally and taking a longer look into the future at what may affect your business helps to avoid unpleasant and possibly fatal surprises. Assessing your overall business environment on at least an annual basis allows you to set effective long-term strategies. A diagram of the planning process illustrates this.

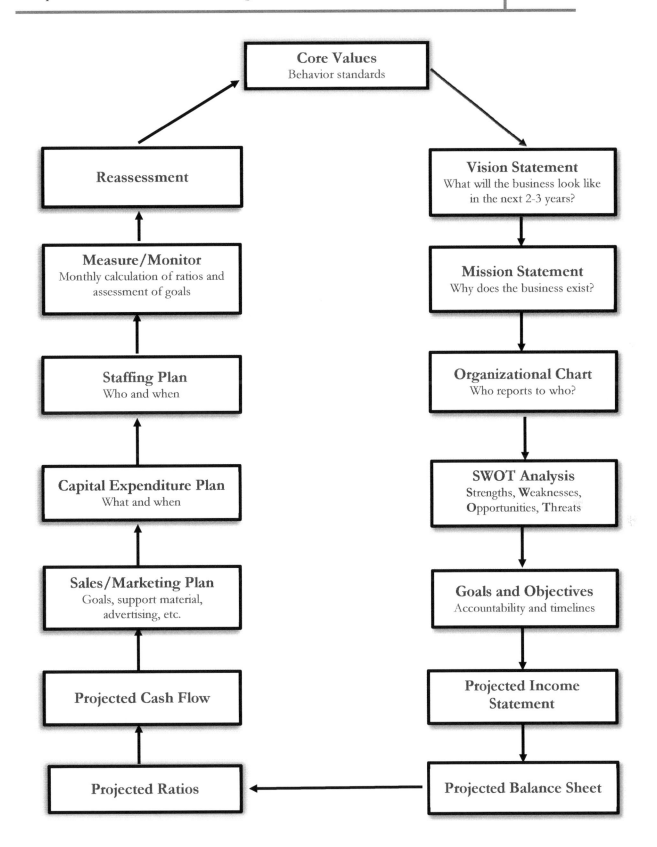

The planning process starts with a definition of the values of the owners and moves toward the establishment of a vision and mission for the company.

CORE VALUES

What does the company stand for? What values drive your company? Once you have established your core values, make sure your employees know what they are. Put up a card in a plastic stand, and put it on every employee's desk. Talk about core values in staff meetings. This is who you are, and these are the values that you want and expect your employees to follow.

VISION STATEMENT

What do you expect the business to look like at the end of three years? Sales? Locations? Services? Once you have your vision statement done, post it in your lobby, conference room, lunch room, and warehouse. Prominently display it where your employees can see it every day. In this way, your employees will know what your vision is, where you are trying to go, and how they can best help you.

MISSION STATEMENT

The mission statement should be a concise one or two paragraph statement that reflects the main purpose or focus of the business. It may answer questions like:

1. Why does the business exist?
2. What does the business *really* do?

You may be surprised how difficult it is to boil the mission of the company down to a couple of sentences, but it is an important part of the planning exercise. You will want to have key employees and selected outsiders review this statement to ensure that it properly reflects the feelings and values of those who are expected to implement it. Once you have your mission statement done, post it in your lobby, conference room, lunchroom, and warehouse. Make sure it is prominently displayed where your employees can see it every day.

In my business we had a one sentence mission statement:

We help businesses achieve financial success.

It is one sentence that explained why we existed. It took us two days to write it.

ORGANIZATIONAL CHART

I have rarely gone into a business and asked for an organizational chart and have one presented. When I do get one, it is very likely either out of date or has people reporting to people that did not seem to make any sense, or in some cases reporting to each other. On more than one occasion I asked if the chart was really how things were from a reporting standpoint and the answer would be "Oh no, that's just we have for public consumption." The fact is that most business owners do not like to prepare formal organizational charts because they want reporting relationships to be more flexible and not tied down to lines and boxes.

I think that this is a mistake. Except for perhaps the smallest businesses, employees should have clearly defined reporting relationships. If one person reports to more than one boss, then it should be clearly spelled out who supervises what. Sometimes a person is involved in both operations and sales and so very well could have two reporting supervisors, as an example.

Organizational charts should be prepared. They should be clear and unambiguous, and they should be updated whenever necessary. If emotions are involved with certain reporting relationships, they should be discussed and resolved. No good can come from sweeping this sort of thing under the rug and hope that no one notices.

SWOT ANALYSIS

The SWOT analysis involves an assessment of both the external and internal environments of the business. The formal term for this process is *environmental scanning*.

The external environmental analysis consists of an assessment of the following items:

1. The competition
2. Legal/regulatory changes
3. The economy
4. The industry
5. Social trends
6. Emerging technology

You are identifying *opportunities* and *threats* that could possibly impact the business. Effective strategies take advantage of the opportunities and do everything possible to minimize the threats.

The internal environment analysis consists of an assessment of the following items:

1. Personnel and management capabilities
2. Physical capacity
3. Financial capacity
4. Products/services offered
5. Sales and marketing
6. Organizational structure

You are establishing a candid assessment of the *strengths* and *weaknesses* that the business may have. Effective strategies take advantage of the strengths and do everything possible to strengthen the weaknesses.

This exercise, referred to as a SWOT analysis, identifies the **s**trengths, **w**eaknesses, **o**pportunities, and **t**hreats in your external and internal environments.

STRATEGIC OBJECTIVES

Setting strategic objectives is the next step, and they are often set in the following areas:

1. Growth rate for sales or profits
2. Diversification plans
3. Updating systems
4. Acquisition plans
5. Market share
6. Implementing new programs

The objectives should be specific, realistic, flexible, measurable, and well documented, and they should have deadlines.

Responsibility for each objective should be assigned to an appropriate person. Establish deadlines. Monitor them carefully to make sure plans, goals, and objectives are on track. This is a key phase of the process. Do not succumb to the temptation to simply put the plan on the shelf and forget about it until the end of the year. Nothing will happen, and you will have wasted a lot of time and effort.

Example:

Objective:	Establish a plan for increasing the leads generated by the website.
Assigned to:	Frank Anderson.
Time Line:	Phase I: preliminary report with initial recommendations and estimated expenses—due February 1.
	Phase II: specific plan presented to management committee—due March 1.
	Phase III: completion—due April 1.

STRATEGIC REVIEW

The only constant in your life and business is change. Nothing remains the same. Take a look at your strengths, weaknesses, opportunities, and threats at least annually. Reassess the overall direction of your business. Refine your vision, mission, goals, and objectives. Make sure you involve the key people in your company. Keep them informed as to where you are going and what you are trying to do.

BENEFITS OF PLANNING

There are many benefits of planning, which include:
1. Encourages management to consider and evaluate basic company policies.
2. Encourages management to look ahead, to consider conditions that are likely to prevail outside the company.
3. Promotes a team concept within the company.
4. Provides for the most effective and economical use of labor, facilities, and capital.
5. Promotes understanding throughout the company of the problems faced by each department.

6. Serves as a means of evaluating progress or lack thereof toward stated goals.
7. Provides a commitment to a plan of action.
8. Instills in management at all levels the habit of carefully considering all factors before making a final decision.
9. Avoids or minimizes costly mistakes or errors in judgment.
10. Maintains the focus of the employees on the stated mission and objectives of the business.

PLANNING TIMETABLE

The following is an approximate timetable for the planning process. Your timetable will be different if your fiscal year-end is not December.

September	Begin to assemble information on the economy and the industry for the coming year. Ask your bank, trade association and CPA for help. Pay attention to what is written in the newspaper and what is said on TV. Use the Internet to help you get a handle on what the coming year looks like economically.
October	Ask your salespeople for their estimates on what they think they can do next year. Look at your numbers at the end of September, and begin to formulate a sales forecast for the coming year.
November	Take your key management off-site for at least a day and formulate your strategic plan and preliminary financial plan.
December	Revise and update your forecasts for the coming year based upon your November numbers.
January	Finalize your strategic and financial plan for the year after you have reviewed your in-house December financial statements.

PLAN CONTENT

The following items should be in your business plan:
I. **Company Overview**
   A. Current year summary—actual performance versus plan, goals achieved, etc.
   B. Outlook for the coming year—economy, industry, and company.
   C. Company profile—a paragraph describing your company.
   D. Financial summary—sales, profits, and key ratios for the past three years.
   E. Core values—what values drive the company?
   F. Vision statement—what the company will look like at the end of three years.
   G. Mission statement—why are you in business?
   H. Organizational chart—who reports to whom?
   I. Current staff levels for administration, sales, operations, production, etc.
II. **Strategic goals and objectives**
   List the primary goals that you hope to accomplish for the coming year, the persons responsible, and their deadlines.

III. **Sales and marketing plan**
    A. Lines of business you hope to grow and how that will be accomplished.
    B. Sales goals by product line, market area, and individual salesperson.
    C. Lead development programs.
    D. Marketing plan—advertising, collateral material, community involvement, etc.
    E. New products/services, if any, that will be offered and the plan for doing that.

IV. **Financial Plan**
    A. Forecasted income statement, including supporting assumptions.
    B. Forecasted balance sheet.
    C. Forecasted cash flow.
    D. Forecasted ratios.
    E. Capital expenditure plan—equipment, timing, and planned financing.

V. **Facilities plan**
    A. Expansion necessary.
    B. Major repairs planned.
    C. Lease renewals required.

VI. **Staff plan**
    A. Layoffs.
    B. New hires.

SUMMARY

Business owners do not like to plan. The phone is always ringing, and it's easy to be consumed by the pressures of the tasks at hand. However, planning for the future is important and well worth the time involved. Your long-term success and survival may depend upon it.

Planning does not *take* time; it *saves* time. You make a decision and set a course of action only once, instead of over and over again. Invest your time and effort into this process, and your business will become more successful. *Writing it down is halfway there.*

For small companies in one location, the planning process will not be as long or as detailed as it will be for larger businesses. For those with sales over ten million dollars and multiple locations, the process will take longer, involve more people, and be more complex.

There are some important aspects of this process:

1. Make sure all the people who will be responsible for achieving the plan are involved in the planning process and are committed to the plan. This should not be a top-down process that is dictated by owners and forced upon key employees.
2. Do not have your planning meeting at the company. There are too many distractions for it to be effective. Go off to a hotel or resort where you will have fewer distractions. Make sure everyone has their computers and phones turned off, and that they don't check e-mail or voice mail during the meeting or at breaks. If necessary, they can check for messages and return calls after the end of the day.

3. Include a social aspect to the meeting–cocktail hour–meals. Give your employees a chance to interact on a non-business basis and get to know each other better. This is the team that will help you achieve success, and the better they know, like, and respect each other, the more successful you will be.

4. Review the progress of the plan monthly. This is not something that should sit on your credenza until the end of the year. It is a dynamic process that needs to be reviewed constantly. Establishing a plan and then ignoring it during the year would be worse than having no plan at all.

The next chapter will begin a discussion of the financial planning process and describe how to project the income statement. Keep on paddling!

CHAPTER TWELVE: PROJECTING THE INCOME STATEMENT

STEPS IN FORECASTING THE INCOME STATEMENT

The first step in establishing your financial plan is projecting the income statement. There are four steps in this process.

1. Forecast sales.
2. Forecast gross profit.
3. Forecast indirect or overhead expenses.
4. Forecast net profit.

FORECAST SALES
A number of factors must be taken into account in this exercise:

1. The status of the economy (national/local)
2. The status of the industry
3. Input from salespeople and key management
4. Historical sales trends
5. Competition
6. Market size and share
7. Financial resources
8. Human resources
9. Physical resources
10. Anticipated changes in technology
11. Regulatory environment
12. Customer preferences/social trends
13. Management and employee input

FORECAST GROSS PROFIT
The gross profit is usually forecast based on a percentage of sales. This percentage should reflect both the historical performance of the business as well as the goals and objectives of management. If you have established standards within your company for the gross profit margin, then the amount of gross profit will be determined by applying that percentage to the forecasted sales.

FORECAST INDIRECT EXPENSES
Indirect operating expenses should be forecast individually on a line-by-line basis. Items such as office expenses may be forecast based on a percentage of sales. Administrative salaries will be forecast based upon projected head count and whether or not you intend to grant any salary increases.

FORECAST NET PROFIT
Other income and expenses are forecast based on historical experience.

CASE STUDY—DURSON DISTRIBUTORS

Allen and his leadership team spent a productive day in a planning meeting outside the business. It was the first ever planning meeting for the company, and it started with an overview of the strengths, weaknesses, opportunities and threats that Durson faced (SWOT analysis). This turned out to be a spirited and candid assessment, and some members of the team had to be reminded occasionally not to take things personally. The result was a gradual increase in the feeling of camaraderie and team spirit as the day progressed.

The CFO then reviewed the financial results for 20X4—20X6 and talked about areas of the business that needed to improve. The VP of sales was particularly taken aback upon hearing some of this information, having felt that the increase in sales under his leadership was nothing short of phenomenal. It took some time and convincing before he was able to understand that too much growth may not be the best strategy from a financial standpoint.

After lunch, Allen spent time discussing the economic and industry conditions that they could expect in 20X7, which was followed by a discussion of the potential sales for 20X7. The consensus was that sales growth in 20X7 should be planned at 10 percent, which produces sales of $14,400. The plan was to be selective and emphasize only the higher profit product lines. Jim Closing, the VP of sales, was not enthusiastic about this strategy, but he ultimately agreed.

The group then turned their attention to expenses. It was decided that the gross profit margin could be improved to 34.5 percent, which was slightly less than what the company had in 20X4. This produced a gross profit of $4,968.

They then spent the rest of the afternoon examining every overhead expense in detail and determined where cuts and efficiencies could be obtained. There was a lot of spirited discussion back and forth as people attempted to protect their favored expenditures, but in the end everyone was surprised and pleased that they arrived at only a 1 percent increase over 20X6, despite a 10 percent forecasted increase in sales.

The CFO then estimated other income, other expenses and interest expense, which produced a net profit of $854 and a stunning net profit margin of 5.9 percent, the highest margin achieved since 20X1.

The leadership team felt proud of what they had accomplished. They had worked hard, learned a lot, and felt closer as a team. They knew where they were going in the coming year and they were all committed to get there. Cocktails and a steak dinner allowed for a relaxed end to the day, and the attendees went home inspired and motivated to have a great year.

The projected income statement for 20X7 is reflected on the following page.

Durson Distributors
Income statement projection 20X7 (000)

	20X4	% Rev	20X5	% Rev	20X6	% Rev	Planned 20X7	% Rev
Sales	$6,555	100.0%	$9,177	100.0%	$13,100	100.0%	$14,400	100.0%
Cost of goods sold	4,274	65.2%	6,048	65.9%	8,725	66.6%	9,432	65.5%
Gross profit	$2,281	34.8%	$3,129	34.1%	$4,375	33.4%	$4,968	34.5%
Advertising	89	1.4%	125	1.4%	180	1.4%	173	1.2%
Bad debts	64	1.0%	81	0.9%	95	0.7%	100	0.7%
Depreciation	70	1.1%	95	1.0%	126	1.0%	115	0.8%
Equipment leases	30	0.5%	61	0.7%	88	0.7%	88	0.6%
Insurance	110	1.7%	150	1.6%	201	1.5%	230	1.6%
Legal and accounting	25	0.4%	31	0.3%	33	0.3%	30	0.2%
Miscellaneous	35	0.5%	46	0.5%	81	0.6%	75	0.5%
Office expenses	48	0.7%	55	0.6%	71	0.5%	68	0.5%
Payroll tax and benefits	200	3.0%	281	3.1%	412	3.1%	421	2.9%
Rent	187	3.2%	210	2.3%	325	2.5%	325	2.3%
Repairs and maintenance	22	0.3%	36	0.4%	31	0.2%	35	0.2%
Salaries	735	11.2%	1,039	11.3%	1,480	11.3%	1,480	10.3%
Sales commissions	172	2.6%	236	2.6%	393	3.0%	432	3.0%
Business tax and license	35	0.5%	60	0.7%	72	0.5%	81	0.6%
Telephone and utilities	48	0.7%	47	0.5%	52	0.4%	45	0.3%
Travel and entertainment	65	1.0%	95	1.0%	147	1.1%	115	0.8%
Vehicle expenses	109	1.7%	152	1.7%	201	1.5%	216	1.5%
Total operating expenses	2,044	31.2%	2,800	30.5%	3,988	30.4%	4,029	28.0%
Operating profit	$237	3.6%	$329	3.6%	$387	3.0%	$939	6.5%
Other income	19	0.3%	21	0.2%	28	0.2%	30	0.2%
Other expenses	(40)	(0.6%)	(55)	(0.6%)	(51)	(0.4%)	(50)	(0.3%)
Interest expense	(47)	(0.7%)	(109)	(1.2%)	(175)	(1.3%)	(62)	(0.4%)
Net profit	$169	2.6%	$186	2.0%	$189	1.4%	$857	6.0%

SUMMARY

Most businesses do not spend much time, if any, preparing a formal plan, despite the significant benefits that can be derived from this exercise. If this includes you, make a pledge that you will make this happen in your company. Your employees want to help you achieve your company's goals, and they therefore need to be aware of what they are. Better yet, they should participate in establishing them. Nothing builds commitment like involvement.

If you have multiple locations, each branch income statement should be forecast, with the participation of the branch manager, and then combined for the overall company's income statement. There is usually a huge, emotional, and largely unproductive debate about how to allocate administrative overhead to each branch. My advice is to not bother. Each branch manager should be held accountable for the expenses over which they have some control, which does not include the overhead expenses of head office. Branches need to make a satisfactory profit margin which contributes to pay the company overhead, and that is what they should focus on. Accountability for the company overhead and the profitability of the company as a whole falls to the CEO, not the branch manager.

Projections of the balance sheet, cash flow, and financial ratios are dependent upon the projected income statement and will be discussed in following chapters. Commit all of this to paper, and then frequently monitor it during the year. In this fashion, both you and your employees will be able to assess the progress towards achieving your financial goals.

When you incorporate a planning meeting and financial planning into your management process, you'll develop the teamwork and financial discipline that is needed to run a successful business and the skills to better anticipate and assess your future performance.

The next chapter will discuss how to project the balance sheet. Keep on paddling!

CHAPTER THIRTEEN: PROJECTING THE BALANCE SHEET

Once you've projected the income statement, the next step in the financial planning process is to project the balance sheet.

Any balance sheet forecast is nothing more than the best guess of those doing the forecasting. If actual results match the forecast to the dollar, it would be a huge coincidence. The goal for projecting the balance sheet is to arrive at numbers that will be reasonably close, given the sales and net profit forecasts. In other words, there is no need to agonize over this process or try to get it down to the exact dollar. What you want is a reasonably close approximation of the balance sheet accounts so that you can forecast cash flow and the financial ratios.

FORECASTING THE BALANCE SHEET

FORECASTING ASSETS

Some of the assets accounts are forecast based upon their historical percentage of sales. The percentage is calculated by dividing the balance of the account at the end of the year by the sales for that year. That percentage is then applied to the forecast sales for the coming year in order to arrive at the end-of-year amount for that account. Prepaid expenses and other current assets are forecast by this percentage of sales method.

Cash is a plug number based on the minimum cash desired in the business. Put in any amount that you feel is appropriate.

Accounts receivable are forecast based upon the desired days sales outstanding. Divide projected sales by 365 to arrive at one day's sales, and then multiply that amount by the desired number of days sales outstanding to calculate year-end accounts receivable.

Inventory days are forecast based upon the number of days desired. Divide cost of goods sold by 365, and then multiply that amount by the desired number of inventory days.

Fixed assets are forecast based upon the capital expenditures planned for the year.

Accumulated depreciation is obtained from the depreciation schedule provided by the CPA.

Other assets are forecast based on the business owner's knowledge of the assets that are contained in this category.

FORECASTING LIABILITIES

The bank line of credit is projected last and will be a balancing item, if needed.

Accounts payable are forecast based on the number of days desired. Divide cost of goods sold by 365, and then multiply that amount by the desired number of payable days.

Accrued Expenses, and other current liabilities are forecast based on their percent of sales, as described for assets above.

Current portion of long-term debt and long-term debt will be obtained from the loan schedule provided by the CPA.

Other long-term liabilities are forecast based on the business owner's knowledge of the liabilities that are contained in this category.

FORECASTING EQUITY

Equity is forecast by adding projected net profit to the prior year's equity, less any income taxes paid or distributions to owners.

SUMMARY OF BALANCE SHEET ACCOUNT FORECASTING

Asset Accounts	Method
Cash	Minimum cash balance desired
Accounts Receivable	Days sales outstanding
Inventory	Inventory days
Prepaid expenses	Percentage of sales
Other current assets	Percentage of sales
Gross fixed assets	From capital expenditure plan
Accumulated depreciation	From depreciation schedule
Other assets	Based on account contents

Liability Accounts	
Line of credit	Balancing number
Accounts payable	Payable days desired
Accrued expenses	Percentage of sales
Other current assets	Percentage of sales
Current portion of long-term debt	Loan schedule
Long-term debt	Loan schedule
Other long-term liabilities	Based on account contents

Steps in forecasting the balance sheet

1. Put in a minimum level of cash desired, maybe $50,000 or more, depending on the size of your business.
2. Divide projected sales by 365 to get sales for one day, and multiply that by the desired days sales outstanding (DSO) to get projected accounts receivable.
3. Determine the percentage of sales for the accounts listed above and multiply that percentage by projected sales to arrive at the year-end projections.
4. Estimate fixed assets based on your equipment needs (cap-ex plan).

5. Determine accumulated depreciation from the depreciation schedule supplied by your CPA, adjusted for new equipment purchases, if any.
6. Establish an amount for other assets based upon account contents (investments, boat, condo, cash value of life insurance, etc.).
7. Add up the asset accounts to determine the amount of total assets, and use that same number for total liabilities and equity.
8. Add the projected net profit, less any income taxes or distributions to owners, to the prior year's equity to get the new equity.
9. Subtract your forecasted equity in step eight from total liabilities and equity to arrive at total liabilities.
10. Subtract long-term debt (from the loan schedules) and other long-term liabilities, if any, from total liabilities to arrive at current liabilities.
11. Determine the current portion of long-term debt from the loan schedule.
12. Determine the accounts payable based upon desired payable days.
13. Determine the accrued expenses, and other current liabilities as a percentage of forecasted sales.
14. The line of credit, if any is needed, is the balancing number for the balance sheet. If no line of credit is needed, use what is leftover to reduce debt, increase cash or make a distribution to owners and reduce equity by that amount.

This process may seem complicated but it is straightforward once you get the hang of it.

The order of things is as follows:

1. Start at the top of the assets and work your way down to total assets.
2. Plug that number into total liabilities and equity.
3. Calculate new equity by adding projected net profit, less income taxes or owner distributions, to the prior year's equity.
4. Subtract the projected equity from total liabilities and equity to arrive at total liabilities.
5. Subtract long-term liabilities (from the loan schedule) from total liabilities to calculate current liabilities.
6. Forecast accrued expenses and other current liabilities as a percentage of sales.
7. Forecast accounts payable based on projected payable days.
8. Determine if an amount is needed for the line of credit in order to balance the balance sheet. If not, increase cash, reduce a liability, or reduce equity by distributing the extra cash out to owners.

This exercise is intended to come reasonably close to what the balance sheet will look like at the end of the forecasted period. It is *not* intended to be exact down to the dollar, and that type of accuracy is not needed. Feel free to round everything off to the nearest thousand.

The following is the projected balance sheet for Durson Distributors, with explanations as to how all of the accounts were determined.

Durson Distributors
Balance sheet projection (000)

	20X4	20X5	20X6	Planned 20X7
Cash[1]	$108	$90	$104	$100
Accounts receivable[2]	845	1,325	1,999	1,400
Inventory[3]	978	1,560	2,601	1,500
Other current assets[4]	55	84	101	115
Current assets	**1,986**	**3,059**	**4,805**	**3,115**
Gross fixed assets[5]	1,301	1,789	2,100	2,100
Accumulated depreciation[6]	(768)	(888)	(1,068)	(1,183)
Net fixed assets	533	901	1,032	917
Other assets[7]	44	52	55	55
Total assets	**$2,563**	**$4,012**	**$5,892**	**$4,087**
Line of credit—bank[8]	194	773	1,436	-0-
Trade accounts payable[9]	560	888	1,619	819
Accrued expenses[10]	45	66	97	101
Current portion long-term bank debt[11]	55	102	118	102
Current liabilities[12]	**854**	**1,829**	**3,270**	**1,022**
Long-term bank debt[13]	423	683	947	825
Shareholder debt[14]	-0-	100	150	150
Total liabilities[15]	**1,277**	**2,612**	**4,367**	**1,997**
Capital stock	75	75	75	75
Retained earnings[16]	1,211	1,325	1,450	2,015
Owner's equity	**1,286**	**1,400**	**1,525**	**2,090**
Total liabilities and equity[17]	**$2,563**	**$4,012**	**$5,892**	**$4,087**

Notes:
1. Plugged at a $100.
2. Forecast at thirty-five days sales outstanding.
3. Forecast at fifty-eight inventory days.
4. Forecast at 0.8 percent of sales.
5. Determined by capital expenditure plans.
6. Obtained from depreciation schedule or determined by adding the coming year's forecasted depreciation to prior year's level.

7. Determined by knowledge of what is contained in this account.
8. A balancing number if needed. It is the last number to be determined in the forecasting of the balance sheet.
9. Forecast at thirty-two payable days.
10. Forecast at 0.7 percent of sales.
11. Obtained from loan schedule.
12. Determined by subtracting long-term liabilities from total liabilities.
13. Obtained from loan schedule.
14. Held over from the prior year per bank requirements.
15. Determined by subtracting equity from total liabilities and equity.
16. Determined by adding forecast net profit less a distribution to owner of $292 (with the permission of the bank) to prior year's retained earnings.
17. Plugged as equal to total assets.

SUMMARY

Projecting the balance sheet might seem complicated or even impossible, but all you need to do is make a few fundamental assumptions, based on questions like:

1. What is the minimum cash that you want on hand at the end of the year?
2. How often do you expect to turn your accounts receivable, inventory, and payables?
3. What is the average of other current assets as a percentage of sales?
4. What capital expenditures do you expect to make in the coming year?
5. What is the average of other current liabilities as a percentage of sales?
6. How much of the forecasted net profit do you expect to distribute to owners?

It is not necessary or possible to forecast the balance sheet to the nearest dollar. This exercise is intended to come up with a reasonable approximation of what the balance sheet will look like at the end of the year, and you should feel free to round off at least to the nearest thousand.

Once the income statement and balance sheet have been forecast, it is a simple matter to calculate the new ratios and cash flow, which will be discussed in the next chapter. Keep on paddling!

CHAPTER FOURTEEN: PROJECTING CASH FLOW AND RATIOS

Projecting cash flow and financial ratios is the final step in the financial planning process. The cash flow and ratios are derived from and are the result of the projected income statement and balance sheet.

CASE STUDY—DURSON DISTRIBUTORS

PROJECTED CASH FLOW

Net profit	$857
Change in current assets less cash	1,686
Change in current liabilities less bank/shareholder debt	(796)
Change in net fixed assets	115
Change in non-current assets	-0-
Equals operating cash flow	**$1,862**

$1,859 \div \$14,400 = 12.91\%$ **= Operating cash flow margin (OpCFM)**

Change in bank debt	($1,574)
Change in shareholder debt	-0-
Change in other long-term debt	-0-
Equity adjustment	(292)
Equals financing cash flow	**($1,866)**

$(\$1,863) \div \$14,400 = (12.94\%)$ **= Financing cash flow margin (FinCFM)**

Operating cash flow	$1,862
Financing cash flow	(1,866)
Equals net cash flow	**($4)**

$(\$4) \div \$14,400 = (0.03\%)$ **= Net cash flow margin (NetCFM)**

PROJECTED RATIOS

The next page reflects the financial ratios and cash flow as forecasted for 20X7.

Durson Distributors
Ratio worksheet

	20X4	20X5	20X6	20X7	Industry Average
Liquidity					
Current ratio	2.33	1.67	1.47	3.05	2.60
Safety					
Debt-to-equity	0.99	1.87	2.86	0.96	1.10
Profitability					
Gross profit margin	34.8%	34.1%	33.4%	34.5%	36.2%
Operating profit margin	3.6%	3.6%	3.0%	6.5%	6.0%
Net profit margin	2.6%	2.0%	1.4%	6.0%	5.0%
Operating Performance					
Return on equity (ROE)	13.1%	13.3%	12.4%	41.0%	29.8%
Days sales outstanding (DSO)	47 days	53 days	56 days	35 days	36 days
Inventory days	84 days	94 days	109 days	58 days	56 days
Payable days	48 days	54 days	68 days	32 days	34 days
Z score	6.1	4.1	3.3	7.6	5.0
Cash Flow					
Operating cash flow margin	(11.1%)	(10.2%)	(7.0%)	12.91%	NA
Financing cash flow margin	7.9%	10.0%	7.1%	(12.94%)	NA
Net cash flow margin	(3.2%)	(0.2%)	0.1%	(0.03%)	NA

The news for 20X7 is all good.

1. Liquidity, as reflected by the current ratio, has improved substantially and is now above the industry average.
2. Safety, as reflected by the debt-to-equity ratio, has improved substantially and is now better than the industry average.
3. Profit margins have all improved substantially, and the operating and net profit margins are both above the industry averages.
4. Return on equity has improved substantially and is now well above the industry average.
5. Days sales outstanding were forecast at thirty-five days and this will be achieved by dedicating a person to calling all of the delinquent accounts.
6. Inventory days were forecast at fifty-eight days and this will be accomplished by monitoring inventory on a regular basis.
7. Accounts payable days were forecast at thirty-two days, and forecasted operating cash flow is sufficient to produce this result.
8. The Z score has improved to above the 20X4 level and exceeds the excellent standard of 5.0.
9. Operating cash flow is a positive $1,863 thanks to the increase in the turnover of accounts receivable and inventory. As assets go *down*, cash flow goes *up*.

10. The strong operating cash flow allowed for a significant reduction in bank and trade debt.

The following is the cash flow worksheet for 20X7.

Cash flow worksheet

Line		20X4	20X5	20X6	20X7
1	Net profit (loss)	169	186	189	857
2	Change in current assets—excluding cash	(830)	(1,091)	(1,732)	1,686
3	Change in current liabilities—excluding bank and shareholder debt	315	319	762	(796)
4	Change in net fixed assets	(338)	(368)	(131)	115
5	Change in noncurrent assets	(12)	(8)	(3)	-0-
6	**Equals operating cash flow**	**(696)**	**(962)**	**(915)**	**1,862**
7	**Operating cash flow margin**	**(10.6%)**	**(10.5%)**	**(7.0%)**	**12.91%**
8	Change in bank/lease debt	574	886	943	(1,574)
9	Change in shareholder debt	-0-	100	50	-0-
10	Change in other long-term debt	-0-	-0-	-0-	-0-
11	Equity adjustment	(88)	(42)	(64)	(292)
12	**Equals financing cash flow**	**486**	**944**	**929**	**(1,866)**
13	**Financing cash flow margin**	**7.4%**	**10.3%**	**7.1%**	**(12.94%)**
14	**Net cash flow—line 6 + line 12**	**(210)**	**(18)**	**14**	**(4)**
15	**Net cash flow margin**	**(3.2%)**	**(0.2%)**	**0.1%**	**(0.03%)**
	Cash flow proof				
16	Prior-period cash from the balance sheet	318	108	90	104
17	+ net cash flow—Line 14	(210)	(18)	14	(4)
18	Equals current-period cash from the balance sheet	108	90	104	100

SUMMARY OF THE FINANCIAL PLANNING PROCESS.

At the end of 20X6, Durson Distributors was in trouble and on the verge of losing their bank financing. Allen Durson had grown the company at a rapid rate and used existing cash, bank debt plus some trade and shareholder debt to finance this growth. Operating cash flow was negative, and there was no one in the company who had any idea that a serious problem was developing until it was almost too late.

This pattern is exactly what happens when a company grows rapidly and no one is monitoring a few key ratios. The focus is on sales. Everyone is working hard, and things like accounts receivable collection, inventory management, and expense control are neglected. I have seen this happen many times, and it is totally avoidable if the principles in this book are employed and growth is carefully managed. No one can grow as fast as they want, because all firms are constrained by available equity.

This case study illustrates that excess growth can be undesirable, and you cannot determine the financial condition of your business by just looking at the *numbers* on your financial statements. You must also look at key *relationships*. You need to know what relationships to look at and why you are looking at them. Profits rarely, if ever, relate to cash flow so you cannot assume that the more you make the more cash you will have.

Establishing your business plan, as outlined in chapters ten through fourteen, provides a blueprint for correcting any financial problems that you might have. This is powerful information that less than 1 percent of all business owners ever have.

Pledge to yourself that you will never end up like Durson in 20X3 or in 20X6. Your goal should be to get to the thunder phase of business *and stay there*. Easier said than done, but with careful planning and management of your financial relationships and by applying the principles contained in this book, you can make this happen. Keep this book on your credenza, and refer to it regularly. Use it or lose it.

20X8—ONE YEAR LATER

At the beginning of 20X7, Allen sat down with his leadership team and designed a profit sharing program based upon sharing any profit over a threshold based on a return on assets (net profit ÷ total assets). A consultant told them that a good return to use for their industry is 10 percent, and that is what they chose as a minimum return for the company. A base net profit was set at $589 (10 percent x total assets of $5,892). They decided to share 50 percent of any profit over $589, which would be shared equally by all employees. They explained this profit sharing program to the employees and then informed them monthly how the company was doing.

When the employees realized that they could make a bonus if the company exceeded the $589 net profit level, they began to focus on how they could help the company become more profitable. In other words, they began to think like owners.

At the end of 20X7 the company had an actual net profit of $965 (exceeding the forecast amount of $854), and $188 went into the profit sharing pool ($965 - $589 x .5). This enabled each of the 62 employees received a check for $3k. This was a meaningful amount of money, and the employees were over-whelmed. Some were tearful when they received their check.

The company won; the employees won; the Durson family won; the trade creditors won; and the bank won. It was a happy holiday party, and the future looked bright for 20X8.

The above type of profit-sharing plan has the advantage of motivating the employees to think like owners. They become highly focused on building the profitability of the company because they realize that they will share in any profits in excess of the threshold. They understand the necessity for the company to make a reasonable profit and they appreciate being able to share in the amount that exceeds the minimum goal. If you do not currently have a formal bonus or profit sharing program, this is one that you might consider. I have seen it work very well with many clients.

SUMMARY

Think about the power of understanding the financial performance of your business on a historical basis. Discovering where you have been and your financial strengths and weaknesses. Determining what you need to do to improve.

Think about the power of going through the planning and forecasting exercise and having your key management involved and committed to achieving the plan. Think about the power of presenting your historical analysis and financial projections to your banker. Probably less than one percent of the bank's customers ever present this type of information.

Your banker will be impressed and feel confident that you know and understand what you are doing from a financial standpoint. Your bank relations will be strengthened, and you will most likely get what you ask for in the way of bank loans, *because you won't ask for something you don't deserve.*

Pledge to start preparing a financial plan if you are not already doing so. Don't worry about the details of the entire process—simply get started. Follow the general guidelines as outlined in this book. Get help from your banker, CPA, and CFO. The important thing is to get started, and make this a routine part of your managing process.

Homework Assignment

Lay out a planning timetable for your business, starting in the fall and finishing soon after the end of the year (assuming you are on a December 31 fiscal year). Consult with your leadership team to determine the attendees, content, and format of your planning meetings. Make sure your sales team is engaged in the process.

If you are reading this book during the first six months of the year, sit down now and lay out a plan for the balance of the year. Any plan is better than no plan. Set realistic goals for your company, and determine what your cash flow and ratios will look like at the end of the year.

If you are reading this book in the second half of the year, calculate three to four years of ratios for your business, and then lay out a planning timetable and conduct your planning sessions.

The case study used throughout this book is fairly typical of those companies that are driven by growth, and it is illustrative of how quickly you can get into serious trouble without an understanding of the financial dynamics of your company. It is also illustrative of how quickly things can be turned around once you understand the basics and adhere to the principles outlined in this book.

Calculate and study the financial ratios discussed in this book on a monthly basis. Know and understand these ratios so well that you don't have to think about what they mean. Make sure your leadership team knows and understands them as well. It will take a while, but once you fully internalize the concepts you will have a powerful tool that will help you become *perpetually profitable*.

The next chapter will be a summary of the financial management process. Keep on paddling!

Financial Ratio Worksheet

	Formula	year____	year____	year____	Industry Average
Liquidity					
Current ratio	current assets / current liabilities				
Safety					
Debt to equity	total liabilities / equity				
Profitability					
Gross profit margin	gross profit / sales				
Operating profit margin	operating profit / sales				
Net profit margin	net profit / sales				
Operating Performance					
Return on equity (ROE)	net profit / equity				
Days sales outstanding (DSO)	365 / accounts receivable turnover				
Inventory days	365 / inventory turnover				
Payable days	365 / accounts payable turnover				
Z score	see below				5.0
Cash Flow					
Operating cash flow margin	operating cash flow / sales				NA
Financing cash flow margin	financing cash flow / sales				NA
Net cash flow margin	sum of cash flow margins				NA

The Z score is calculated as follows:

Current assets minus current liabilities / Total assets	x 6.56 =	xx
Equity / Total assets	x 3.26 =	xx
Profit before interest and taxes / Total assets	x 6.72 =	xx
Equity / Total liabilities	x 1.05 =	xx

Total   **xxx**

Grading

0–1.0 Very bad
1.1–2.0 Poor
2.1–3.0 Fair
3.1–4.0 Good
4.1–5.0 Very good
5.0+   Excellent

Cash Flow Worksheet

Line		Note	Year	Year	Year
1	Net profit (loss)	1			
2	Change in current assets—excluding cash	2			
3	Change in current liabilities—excluding bank and shareholder debt	3			
4	Change in net fixed assets	4			
5	Change in noncurrent assets	5			
6	**Equals operating cash flow**	6			
7	Operating cash flow margin	7			
8	Change in bank/lease debt	8			
9	Change in shareholder debt	9			
10	Change in other long-term debt	10			
11	Equity adjustment	11			
12	**Equals financing cash flow**	12			
13	Financing cash flow margin	13			
14	**Net cash flow—line 6 + line 12**	14			
15	Net cash flow margin	15			
	Cash flow proof				
16	Prior-period cash from the balance sheet	16			
17	+ net cash flow—Line 14	17			
18	Equals current-period cash from the balance sheet	18			

Notes:
1. Enter net profit or loss from the current-period income statement.
2. Always subtract the current-period from the prior-period to calculate this change.
3. Always subtract the prior-period from the current-period to calculate this change.
4. Always subtract the current-period from the prior-period to calculate this change.
5. Always subtract the current-period from the prior-period to calculate this change.
6. Operating cash flow equals the sum of lines 1–5.
7. Divide operating cash flow on line 6 by sales to calculate the operating cash flow margin (OpCFM).
8. Always subtract the prior-period from the current-period to calculate this change.
9. Always subtract the prior-period from the current-period to calculate this change.
10. Always subtract the prior-period from the current-period to calculate this change.
11. Subtract current-period net profit and prior-period equity from current-period equity to get the equity adjustment.
12. Financing cash flow equals the sum of lines 8–11.
13. Divide financing cash flow on line 12 by sales to calculate the financing cash flow margin (FinCFM).
14. Net cash flow is the sum of operating cash flow and financing cash flow, line 6 and line 12.
15. Divide net cash flow on line 14 by sales to calculate the net cash flow margin (NetCFM).
16. Cash from the prior-period balance sheet.
17. Net cash flow from line 14.
18. The sum of lines 16 and 17 that must equal cash on the current-period balance sheet.

CHAPTER FIFTEEN: FINANCIAL MANAGEMENT SUMMARY

REVIEW OF FINANCIAL MANAGEMENT PRINCIPLES

Let's review a few of the important principles that have been covered earlier in this book.

NUMBERS
1. Effective financial analysis is neither mysterious nor complicated.
2. Most business owners confine their analysis to "How much sales did I have? and "How much profit did I have?" I don't have accurate statistics, but my experience is that maybe 1-2 percent of all business owners do much more than this.
    a. You have to look at key *relationships*, called ratios, in addition to the *numbers*. Your profit *in relationship to something else* is what is important.
    b. You need to look at the *trend* of your ratios over a period of years. Are you good and getting better, or are you bad and getting worse?
    c. You should always compare your ratios to industry averages if they are available. Risk Management Associates (RMA) publishes averages for numerous industries every year. Ask your banker or librarian for this publication to see if your industry is one that is included.
    d. It is important for you to establish your own standards for ratios after you have sufficient experience and history for them. Your goal should be to run an excellent company and exceed the industry averages.

RELATIONSHIPS
3. The balance sheet is a pretty boring document (no sales or profits) and gets little or no attention, but the fact is that a strong balance sheet is the foundation of your business and is therefore very important.
4. Ratios for liquidity, ability to pay bills, and safety, ability to withstand adversity, are used to measure the strength of the balance sheet.
    a. Liquidity is measured by the current ratio, and it is the most important ratio that you calculate because if you can't pay your bills you won't stay in business long.
    b. Working capital is defined as current assets minus current liabilities, and all businesses need adequate working capital.
    c. Safety is measured by the debt-to-equity ratio, and it is your banker's favorite ratio because it is a measurement of the riskiness of your business. Banks do not want to loan money to overly risky businesses.

PROFIT MARGINS
5. The strength of the income statement is measured by the gross profit margin, the operating profit margin, and the net profit margin.

    a. The gross profit margin is the second most important ratio that you will calculate (after the current ratio) because if you get this wrong it is hard to make it up below that line.

    b. Once a few key relationships have been calculated, areas of your business that might need improvement are very easy to spot and corrective action is usually obvious.

PHASES OF BUSINESS

6. There are four distinct phases of business; wonder, blunder, thunder, and plunder. Your goal should be to get to the thunder phase *and stay there*. That may seem obvious, but it takes effective leadership and careful attention to the financial management of the business to accomplish. Your ratios are most likely going to be different depending upon the phase of business you are in.

CASH FLOW

7. Cash is king, and there are two types of cash flows discussed in this book; operating cash flow and financing cash flow. They are extremely important, easy to calculate, and easy to forecast.

    a. Cash flow has little or no relationship to profit. You can have lots of profit and no cash flow (sales and profit are increasing and so are assets causing cash to go down), and you can have lots of cash flow and no profit (sales are declining and assets are decreasing causing cash to go up).

    b. Cash is what you use to pay everything so there needs to be as much focus on cash flow as there is on profit.

    c. From a cash flow standpoint, assets are *bad* (that is they *take* cash) and liabilities are *good* (that is they *supply* cash).

    d. Business owners tend to think that they would be very happy if they could be assured that sales and profits would double every year, which is disastrous in most instances. It is the fastest way to "grow broke" that I know. Too much of anything is usually a bad thing.

    e. Growth needs to be carefully managed. No business can grow as fast as it wants to. All companies are constrained by the amount of capital that they have, and the availability of trained and qualified employees.

WHY SHOULD I BOTHER WITH ALL OF THIS?

There are approximately 28 million small businesses (defined by the SBA as having 500 or fewer employees) in the United States, and if my estimates are correct that only 2 percent bother with this analysis, that means that over 27 million of them are not doing much in the way of financial management or analysis. Since they seem to be doing OK, you might be wondering why you should bother with this.

There are several reasons that come to mind:

1. They are all *not* doing OK. 75 percent of them fail within the first 15 years of their existence. Many of those that have not failed are at best mediocre in their performance

and are not really worth the effort or capital required to keep them going. The great majority of those businesses fail, not due to bad economic or industry conditions, but due to bad management, which largely translates into bad *financial* management. When I owned a company I know that if I had understood all of the principles outlined in this book, both management and financial, I would have been more successful.

Your goal should be to own and/or run an *excellent* business, and not settle for being mediocre or even average. Unless you practice effective leadership and calculate the key relationships outlined in this book on a regular basis it is highly unlikely that you will achieve excellence.

2. The ratios listed in this book, when calculated and reviewed regularly, will act as warning signals if you are heading in the wrong direction. Think of them as similar to the gauges in your car. If the "engine needs attention" light or the "low tire pressure" light comes on, you know that something is wrong well in advance so that you can take corrective action before it becomes a serious problem. If the "oil pressure warning" light comes on, pull over to the side of the road and shut off the engine.

   Ignoring these signals is not wise, but you have to have them in the first place in order to know that there is a problem. That's what the ratios in this book do for you. In most instances, you can identify the problems in plenty of time to take corrective action.

3. There is nothing mysterious, difficult, or time consuming about regularly tracking these ratios. Download the software available on my website, www.leadtosucceed.biz, and all of the calculations will be done for you after you have put in your monthly financial information.

4. Owning and operating a business is a life-long learning exercise. The people who get this right are the ones who are willing to never stop learning and growing, and never believe that they "know it all." They are always asking questions and then listening to the answers. They are true students of the game, and they are successful, stimulating, and enjoyable to be around. Be one of them.

STRIVE TO OPTIMIZE

You may be tempted to think that if a little liquidity is good, then more is better. If a little safety is good, then more is better. If a little sales growth is good, then more is better. This all sounds right but it is not. You need to find the level which is optimal for your business and not try to maximize or minimize anything. Optimize is what you need to do.

OPTIMAL LIQUIDITY
The current ratio, which measures liquidity and is defined as current assets divided by current liabilities is very important, but a higher ratio is not necessarily better than a lower ratio. On a very general basis, a ratio of 2.00 is very good. That would mean $2.00 of current assets to pay every $1.00 of current liabilities. It is a very liquid situation. Is 3.00 better? Not necessarily, but it is more liquid.

A very high current ratio is going to indicate a very high cash position and that is not necessarily desirable for at least three reasons:

1. Cash, even if it is invested in a CD or money market fund, is a very low income producing asset.
2. Excess cash that is not immediately needed in the business can and should be distributed to owners who can invest it more profitably. If the business needs the cash at some future time it can always be loaned back to the business, with interest being paid to the owner.
3. If the business experiences a large calamity that is not completely covered by insurance, cash sitting on the balance sheet is a welcome target by aggressive attorneys in a law suit.

To some extent, your optimal current ratio will be determined by your philosophy on paying bills. If you want to pay a bill the moment it hits your desk, then you are going to need a higher current ratio than if you pay the bill the day it is due or if you only pay the bill when the creditor calls you (not something I would recommend).

A 2.00 current ratio is good. Is 2.20 better? Not necessarily, but it is more liquid. Is 1.90 OK? Yes in most instances. Is 1.75 OK? Yes in most instances. Is 1.25 OK? No, not in most instances. Somewhere between 1.50 and 2.00 is what you should strive for in order to ensure that you have adequate liquidity and working capital.

I once had a client tell me that they needed at least $2,000,000 in the bank in order for them to sleep well at night. I told them that was not a good financial decision, but I can't argue that a good night's sleep is unimportant.

Determine the amount of liquidity that is optimal for your emotional and financial situation and then keep it there. Working capital is important, and excellent companies pay their bills when they are due.

OPTIMAL SAFETY
Safety, the ability to withstand adversity, is obviously important. Adversity can strike at any time, and you want to be in a position to survive. Safety is measured by the debt-to-equity ratio, and the lower this ratio the safer you are. That does not mean that a lower ratio is better, just safer. On a very general basis 1.00 is good. That would mean $1.00 in debt for every $1.00 in equity, or the creditors have the same amount invested in the business as does the owner.

Several factors are going to dictate the optimal degree of safety of your business.

1. Risk tolerance.
Entrepreneurs and business owners are usually bigger risk takers than the general population, but this is an emotional rather than a financial decision, and everyone has their own way of thinking about this. When I left my relatively safe job as a bank vice president to start my own business, my mother, who was a product of the great depression, was appalled. She thought I

was crazy to even think about it. I saw it differently because I felt that we had a good plan and good prospects for success and it was not that risky.

Risk tolerance is likely to change with age and personal circumstances however. If I had been sixty-two instead of forty-two at the time I had the opportunity to start a business, or if I had been saddled with ten kids and a huge mortgage, I probably would not have done it. Everyone has to decide how much risk they are comfortable with, and this is probably a moving target.

2. Type of industry.

Some industries are more leveraged than others. Automobile dealers or other businesses that borrow to invest in their inventory have debt-to-equity ratios that are routinely 5.00 or higher. Motels and other real estate type businesses have high debt-to-equity ratios because they are mortgaged. Restaurants, particularly those that are newly established, tend to have higher debt-to-equity ratios. This does not mean that they are not more risky however, and it is one of the reasons that you see these types of businesses failing when there is a big downturn in the economy. It is not because they are *inherently* riskier types of businesses, it is because they have a high debt-to-equity ratio at the time of the adversity.

Automobile dealerships, motels and restaurants that have been established for a long period of time and have paid off a lot of their debt are the ones that are the most likely to survive.

3. Status of the economy.

If the economic indicators are favorable and all of the gurus are talking about how great things are going to be, then it may be a time to grow the company and take on more debt to do so. On the other hand, economic forecasters often talk about an impending downturn for months before it happens and this information may indicate that it is time to begin paying off debt and improving your safety. In other words, a higher debt-to-equity ratio (and less safety) may be OK if the economic outlook is very good, and the reverse is true.

4. Phase of business.

Startup companies in the wonder and blunder phases of business are going to have more risk and higher debt-to-equity ratios than more established businesses in the thunder and plunder phases. It goes with the territory. The good news is that most businesses survive those early days by a combination of hard work, determination, sweat equity, and maybe a little luck. While it is true that 75 percent of them ultimately fail, the causes of those failures tend to be bad management and failing to follow the tenets and principles outlined in this book, rather than the lack of initial capital (equity).

5. How you were raised.

Dad always said that owing anyone anything was bad. He was smart and he was successful, and you believed him. Enough said.

A debt-to-worth ratio of 1.00 is good. Is 0.75 *better*? Not necessarily, but it is *safer*. Is 1.10 bad? Not necessarily, but it is a little less safe. For most businesses, when you cross the 3.00 debt-to-equity threshold (the creditors have three times more invested in the business that does the owner) you are going to attract special attention at the bank (unless you are in an industry like those listed above that typically have higher debt-to-equity ratios on average). This is seldom desirable. Depending on the averages for your industry, you should strive for somewhere between 1.00 and 2.00.

Take into account the above factors and then determine the optimal degree of safety for your business.

Remember this principle:

To risk nothing is to risk everything.

OPTIMAL PROFITABILITY

It is often said that it is impossible to be too rich or too thin, and most business owners believe that profitability has to be in that category….it is not. Of course it is possible to be too thin, and if you are as rich as Bill Gates your life gets pretty complicated because every whacko out there wants to kidnap you or your family. Maybe it's worth it, but maybe not. What I can say with some certainty is that it is possible to be too profitable. You may think that this statement *cannot* be correct, but let me explain.

I have graphically illustrated in chapter nine what can happen to a business that pursues growth and profits without any notion of the overall financial condition of the business (see chapter nine). Just because some profits are good, that does not necessarily mean that more profits are better.

There are some ways to maximize profitability that may be harmful to the business. Hiring cheap labor, working them hard and turning them over frequently, will increase profits in the short-term but probably hurt in the long-term. Profits can be increased in the short-term by avoiding preventive maintenance or cutting advertising and marketing budgets, both of which can have undesirable long-term consequences.

Actually reducing profits may be beneficial. There are times when you have to spend money to make money, and perhaps lower your profit margins in the short-term in order to build future increased profitability.

Make no mistake, good profitability is at the very heart of your business and it needs to be there. If you are not sufficiently profitable you will not have the necessary funds to reinvest in your business, and you will not be making a sufficient return on investment that is commensurate with the degree of risk that you are taking. In that instance you would be better off to liquidate the whole thing and invest your money elsewhere.

Optimal profitability for your business is unique to your situation and is therefore not something that I can spell out for you in this book. It is going to be determined by measuring the gross, operating, and net profit margins (see chapter six) and establishing what they *should* be. This is the result of several factors:

1. What they have been historically

2. What others in your industry are accomplishing
3. The condition of your industry
4. The condition of the economy
5. The degree of competition you face
6. Your pricing strategy—high cost, low volume versus low cost, high volume, etc.
7. Supply and demand
8. Current fads

You need to be profitable and you should strive to determine your optimal profit margins within the context of the above factors. Then you need to faithfully track them and strive to keep them at the level that you have determined to be appropriate.

If you optimize your balance sheet and income statement ratios, you are almost certainly going to have optimal operating performance and cash flow ratios, and you are going to have good financial health.

CAUSE AND EFFECT ANALYSIS

When one body exerts a force on a second body, the second body simultaneously exerts a force equal in magnitude and opposite in direction on the first body.—Sir Isaac Newton.

That Isaac was a pretty smart dude. When you do something in one area of your business, there tends to be an equal and opposite reaction in another area.

Profitability is at the heart of your business. Remember that I have defined net profit as the bottom line of your income statement before income tax (only *C* corporations pay income tax. *S* corporations, LLCs, sole proprietorships and partnerships do not pay income tax directly. Income tax liability flows through to the owners of the business).

In chapter six I talked about three levels of measuring profitability:

> Sales
> Less direct expenses
> **Gross profit**   *level 1*
> Less overhead expenses
> **Operating Profit**   *level 2*
> Plus other income/expense
> Less interest expense
> **Net profit**   *level 3*

If you study the cause and effect diagram on the following page you will see the two things, high interest and low operating profit margin, that are the cause of a low net profit margin. You will also see how it all relates to cash flow, safety and liquidity.

FINANCIAL ANALYSIS CAUSE & EFFECT DIAGRAM©

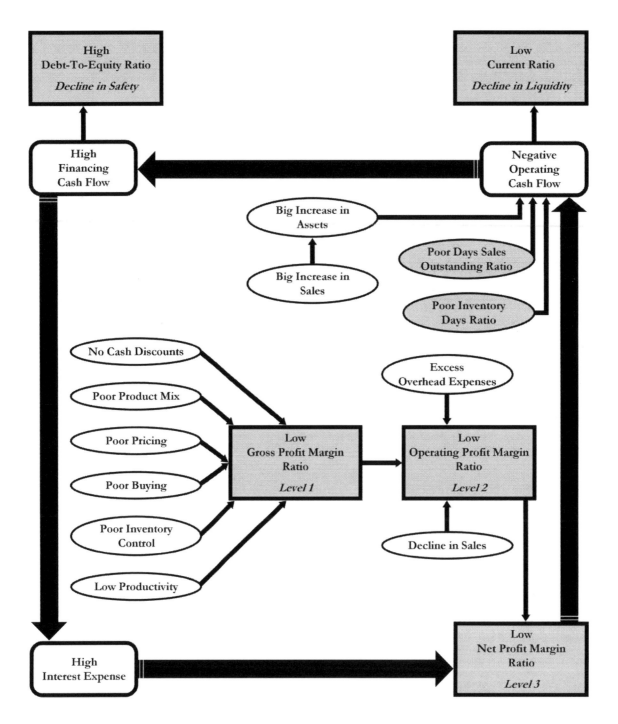

INSTRUCTIONS FOR USING THE CAUSE AND EFFECT DIAGRAM

I know, it's a lot of lines and a lot of arrows and a lot of boxes. The best thing would be for you to stare at it for a while, and not worry about figuring it all out. There are causes, effects, and relationships to everything that we have discussed so far in this book, and the diagram is an attempt to visually show you how all of the financial analysis principles interact.

What you will notice is that the base of the line comes from the *cause* and the point of the arrow is at the *effect*.

It doesn't matter where you start on the diagram, but look at the lower right hand corner and see the Low Net Profit Margin box, that I call level 3. Coming into this box are two arrows, one from the Low Operating Profit Margin box (the cause), and a fat one from the High Interest Expense box (the cause). What this is indicating is that there are two possible causes for a low net profit (the effect); either a low operating profit or high interest expense.

Follow the thin arrow line back to the low operating profit box and you see that there are three possible causes for a low operating profit; decline in sales, excess overhead expenses, and a low gross profit.

Follow the thin arrow line back some more and you will see that there are six possible causes for a low gross profit; no cash discounts, poor product mix, poor pricing, poor buying, poor inventory control, and low productivity.

So if you are experiencing a low net profit or even a loss, you can trace the arrows back and see that there are two possible causes at level 1 and level 2, and there are eight causes for those two levels. You can then think about each one and see if it might fit your situation. Measuring profitability at levels 1, 2, and 3 is discussed in chapter six.

Trace the fat arrow line on the left hand side of the diagram from High Interest Expense (the effect) up to High Financing Cash Flow (the cause). High financing cash flow is the cause and high interest is the effect. Trace the fat arrow across the top of the diagram to the right and you will see that the cause of High Financing Cash Flow is Negative Operating Cash Flow. Both of these cash flow types are discussed in chapter eight.

Cash is king, and if you trace the thin arrow lines back from the negative operating cash flow box you will see that there are three possible causes for negative operating cash flow; poor inventory days, poor days sales outstanding, and a big increase in assets, which you will see in turn is caused by a big increase in sales. Inventory days and days sales outstanding are discussed in chapter seven. What happens when sales grow at a fast rate is discussed in chapter nine.

Tracing the fat arrow on the right hand side of the diagram downward brings us right back to where we started in the lower right hand corner of the diagram.

The two grey boxes in the upper left and upper right of the diagram are measurements of the strength of your balance sheet. Negative operating cash flow will cause a low current ratio (which is a measurement of your liquidity) and high financing cash flow will cause a high debt-to-equity ratio (which is a measurement of your safety). These ratios are discussed in chapter five.

The four fat lines indicate that the whole thing is a circular process. One thing causes another thing that causes another thing that causes another thing and it all goes around and around, perpetuating itself until someone, probably your banker or your trade creditors, calls a halt to it all. That was clearly illustrated in chapter nine that described an unpleasant meeting of Julian, Allen and their banker in the bank's conference room.

Stare at the diagram. Trace the arrows backward from effect to cause. Go back and re-read some of the chapters if necessary. Eventually, you will come to an understanding about what causes what and how all of this interrelates. Just stare at it and give it a little time to soak in.

Profitability is at the heart of your business and without it you can't survive, so let's take a closer look at the three levels that are indicated on the diagram.

LEVEL 1 PROFITABILITY ANALYSIS

Level 1 is the gross profit margin, and it is what I call the *front line of attack* in your profitability war. Lose the war at level 1 and it is hard to win at levels 2 or 3.

As you can see, there are six possible causes of a low gross profit margin:

1. **No cash discounts.**
   If you have the opportunity to take a cash discount, like paying in ten days with a 2 percent discount instead of thirty days with no discount (2-10, net 30), you should do it. Otherwise, you are effectively paying a 37% interest rate for being able to pay the invoice in 30 days, rather than in 10 days. This is a big cost for holding on to your cash for an additional twenty days and will contribute nicely to increasing your gross profit margin. You need adequate liquidity to do this.

2. **Poor product mix.**
   Most firms have various products or services and all of them probably have different gross profit margins. Theoretically it would make sense only to offer the products or services that have the highest profit margins, but it usually doesn't work that way. You offer some products because it helps you to sell others, or the products or services you offer may have different peak times during the year which keeps you busy year around and more profitable.

3. **Poor pricing.**
   Many firms do not know their costs to produce a particular product or service. It is easy to determine the overall cost of goods sold, but breaking it down to a particular product or service can get complicated. The result is that they tend to either follow the competitors pricing (who also

probably don't know their costs) or they price things the way they always have. Those are two fairly poor reasons to set prices, and the result may be a lower gross profit margin than could otherwise be obtained.

4. **Poor buying.**

Purchasing from the same vendor for a long period of time without getting other bids is usually a mistake. Not taking a cash discount, if offered, is a mistake. Both lead to a lower gross profit margin.

5. **Poor inventory control.**

Inventory needs to be monitored closely and kept in a secure place in order to avoid shrinkage. High inventory levels can cause high carrying costs and lead to obsolescence. Both shrinkage and obsolescence can cause a lower gross profit margin.

6. **Low productivity and/or inflated labor rates**.

The process of delivering a product or service needs to be as efficient as possible. Poor efficiency and/or inflated direct labor rates will lead to excess labor expense and thus a lower gross profit margin. Labor ratios to produce a product or service should be calculated and monitored on a regular basis.

Examine all aspects of your direct expenses, and make sure that you know exactly what each expense should be as a percent of sales. If a particular expense increases even 0.1 percent make sure you know why. If it is unavoidable, try to cover the additional expense with a corresponding price increase.

If you win the profitability war at level 1, then you have a much better chance of winning the battles at levels 2 and 3.

LEVEL 2 PROFITABILITY ANALYSIS

Level 2 is the operating profit margin and it is a function of the amount of overhead expenses that are subtracted from the gross profit. In my experience, most business owners do not have any kind of a detailed knowledge of what these expenses actually are and whether or not they are really necessary. I have never seen a firm, even ones that are well-managed, that could not cut at least 10 percent of their overhead expenses as a result of a detailed analysis of each expense.

Take the time to sit down with your CFO or accounting manager and go over each expense category listed on your income statement on a detailed basis so that you can determine which ones can be cut or reduced. Every dollar you save at this level drops directly to level 3.

If sales decline, as they did for many firms during the great recession of 2008, this leads to a decline in the operating profit margin because business owners are reluctant to cut overhead expenses quickly. The first effort is to try and restore sales to their prior level rather than cut staff or other expenses. This goes on, sometimes for months, before any action is taken to cut expenses, and the result is a steadily declining operating profit margin. If plan A is to increase sales, always make sure that you have a plan B to implement on a timely basis if that does not work.

LEVEL 3 PROFITABILITY ANALYSIS

Level 3 is the net profit margin, and the most significant deduction from your operating profit is most likely going to be interest expense.

Looking at the cause and effect diagram, you can see that a high increase in sales causes a big increase in assets, which causes a negative operating cash flow (as assets go *up*, cash goes *down*), which causes high financing cash flow, which causes high interest expense, which causes a low net profit margin, which in turn causes more negative operating cash flow, which in turn cause a low current ratio (low liquidity) and a high debt-to-equity ratio (low safety). Around and around we go, where she stops nobody knows. Remember that Isaac dude!

Negative operating cash flow is going to cause a decline in liquidity and high financing cash flow is going to cause a decline in safety. All of this is interrelated; the income statement, the balance sheet and cash flow.

Study this cause and effect diagram. Understand what happens to you when sales increase or decrease and why profit margins decline. Relate this to your own business and see where you may need to improve.

If you are a service business and do not have direct and indirect expenses on your income statement, correct this immediately. Without this income statement format you will not know what your level 1 performance is, or more important, what it *should* be. Therefore if your level 3 performance is not adequate you will not know whether it is a problem with the gross profit margin or the operating profit margin, because you do not have them separately stated. As a result, you will be paddling without knowing the direction you need to travel, because correcting a low gross profit margin is a lot different procedure than cutting overhead in order to correct a low operating profit margin. You *have* a gross profit margin and you have *always* had a gross profit margin, you just don't know what it is. This is not good and it is easy to correct.

SUMMARY

There are a lot of numbers in this book, but this book is not about the numbers. It is about leadership and it is about calculating a few financial relationships so that you can know and understand where you have been and, more important, where you are going.

The process of financial management is neither complicated nor time consuming, but without some effort on your part it will not work. Having just read this book it is all fresh in your mind and you have at least a basic understanding of what to do and how to do it, but if you put this book down and never refer to it again it will all be lost in a fairly short period of time.

You should be motivated to do this analysis because the financial relationships that I have presented act as warning signals if something is getting out of line. Areas needing improvement are easy to spot, and in most instances the solutions are pretty obvious. A 75 percent failure rate within fifteen years of being in business should be enough of a motivator, because I guarantee you that if most of those business owners had adhered to the tenets outlined in this book they would still be in business.

Think about the jobs and money lost, and the heartache and disappointment of failure. Of course some businesses should never start in the first place because they don't have a service or product that enough people want, but my guess is that is a very small minority. Study this book and you are not going to fail, and better yet, you will run an excellent company and be perpetually profitable. Make a copy of this book available to your leadership team and make sure they all understand it as well. You will do a lot better if everyone is paddling in the canoe!

Think about optimizing relationships rather than maximizing or minimizing them. I know that there are fancy and complicated mathematical models that are devoted to optimization, but those are not necessary (for which we should all be grateful). Look at your history and consider your personal feelings and beliefs and then set your optimal numbers. It is common sense, and you do not need an advanced degree in mathematics for this exercise.

Remember Sir Isaac. For every action there is an equal and opposite reaction. Study the cause and effect diagram until you *feel* it without having to think about it. One thing leads to another thing which leads to another thing which leads to another thing. I wish for you that it was not true, but it is. Understand the consequences of your actions (or lack thereof) and you will be able to stay out of trouble. Your employees certainly *feel* when things are not going well. Morale declines and that exacerbates an already bad situation (which is another box we could put on the diagram that causes low net profit). Employee morale isn't on the chart, but it is both a cause and an effect when a business is not doing well.

Success is not pre-destined but it is certainly possible. Read this book regularly. Use it or lose it. What gets measured gets managed, and what gets managed gets fixed.

The next chapter will discuss expense behavior and how to determine your break-even sales level. Keep on paddling!

CHAPTER SIXTEEN: EXPENSE BEHAVIOR ANALYSIS

In chapter six, we examined the income statement, and we discussed the importance of separating expenses into direct (cost of goods sold) and indirect (overhead or general and administrative expense). In other words, we classified them by *type* of expense. This allows you to determine your gross profit (sales minus direct expenses) and gross profit margin (gross profit divided by sales). The gross profit margin is one of the most important ratios that you calculate.

In this chapter we define expenses by how they *behave* and separate them into either fixed or variable expense. This is a useful exercise, because a firm grasp of how your expenses behave will help you to determine how best to maximize profits.

EXPENSE BEHAVIOR PATTERNS

FIXED EXPENSES
Fixed expenses are those that do not go up or down with sales. Examples include rent, depreciation, insurance, administrative salaries, and utilities. Obviously if sales go up substantially, then all of these expenses are likely to go up as well, but they do not vary on an incremental basis with sales.

VARIABLE EXPENSES
Variable expenses are caused by sales or tend to go up or down with sales. Examples include direct wages, inventory expense, bad debts, and sales commissions.

Some expenses, such as vehicle operating expenses, contain both fixed (depreciation and license) and variable (fuel, tires, repairs) components. Depreciation should be classified as a fixed expense, and the balance of vehicle operating expenses can be classified as variable.

All of your direct expenses are not variable, and all of your indirect expenses are not fixed. If you are not sure whether an expense is fixed or variable, always classify it as fixed. This will give you a higher break-even sales level and therefore be a more conservative estimate.

DETERMINING BREAK-EVEN SALES

The break-even sales level is determined by the following four steps:

1. Separate expenses into fixed and variable.
2. Subtract variable expenses from sales to determine the contribution margin.
3. Divide the contribution margin by sales to get the contribution margin ratio (CMR).
4. Divide fixed expenses by the contribution margin ratio (CMR).

STEP ONE: SEPARATE EXPENSES INTO FIXED AND VARIABLE

The following is a typical breakdown of fixed and variable expenses.

Fixed Expenses	Variable Expenses
Depreciation	Direct wages
Rent	Employee benefits and taxes[1]
Advertising	Vehicle operating expenses
Employee benefits and taxes[2]	Inventory
Insurance	Bad debts
Legal and accounting	Commissions
Office expense	
Other administrative expense	
Administrative salaries	
Selling and promotion expenses	
Taxes and licenses	
Telephone and utilities	
Travel and entertainment	
Interest[3]	

1. Based on direct wages.
2. Based on administrative salaries.
3. Interest could go up as sales go up and the company borrows more money, however it is included in fixed expenses in order to be conservative. Do not include other income or other expense in this analysis.

STEP TWO: DETERMINE THE CONTRIBUTION MARGIN

The contribution margin is determined by subtracting variable expenses from sales, as follows:

> Sales
> (Variable expenses)
> Contribution margin

The contribution margin is the amount of money that you have left, after paying variable expenses, to pay fixed expenses.

STEP THREE: CALCULATE THE CONTRIBUTION MARGIN RATIO (CMR)

The contribution margin ratio (CMR) is determined by dividing the contribution margin by sales, as follows:

$$\frac{\text{Contribution Margin}}{\text{Sales}} = \text{Contribution Margin Ratio (CMR)}$$

The contribution margin ratio is expressed as a percentage of sales.

STEP FOUR: DIVIDE FIXED EXPENSES BY THE CMR
The break-even sales level is calculated by dividing fixed expenses by the CMR, as follows:

$$\frac{\text{Fixed expenses}}{\text{Contribution margin ratio}} = \text{Break-even sales}$$

CASE STUDY: DURSON DISTRIBUTORS

Step one is separating expenses into fixed and variable and the following are the variable and fixed expenses for 20X6. Note that other income and other expenses are not included in this analysis.

20X6	20X6	Fixed	Variable
Sales	$13,100		
Cost of goods sold			8,725
Advertising		180	
Bad debts			95
Depreciation		126	
Equipment leases		88	
Insurance		201	
Legal and accounting		33	
Miscellaneous		81	
Office expense		71	
Payroll tax and benefits		412	
Rent		325	
Repairs and maintenance		31	
Salaries		1,480	
Sales commissions			393
Business tax and licenses		72	
Telephone and utilities		52	
Travel and entertainment		147	
Vehicle expense		201	
Interest expense[1]		175	
Total		3,675	9,213

[1] Exclude other income and other expense from this analysis. Include only interest expense.

At first blush you may think that some of the expenses, such as advertising, are misclassified. Theoretically the more you advertise the more you sell, so advertising could be considered a variable expense. Advertising is a budgeted fixed amount for the year and does not go up if sales go up. In fact, if sales are very strong, you might even reduce advertising. Some expenses, such as interest, are going to have both a fixed and variable component, however if there is any question, the choice should always be to consider the expense fixed. This will reflect a higher break-even sales level and be the most conservative calculation. Expenses like bad debts and commissions are clearly variable. The more you sell the more accounts receivable you will have, and the more bad debts (on average) you will have.

Step two is determining the contribution margin.

Sales	$13,100
Variable expenses	(9,213)
Contribution margin	$3,887

Step three is to divide the contribution margin by sales to determine the contribution margin ratio (CMR).

$$\frac{\text{Contribution Margin—3,887}}{\text{Sales—13,100}} = 29.67\%$$

The final step is to divide fixed expenses by the contribution margin ratio in order to calculate the level of sales at which the company will exactly break-even, i.e. zero net profit.

$$\frac{\text{Fixed expenses—3,675}}{\text{CMR—.2967}} = \text{Break-even sales—\$12,374}$$

We can verify this calculation as follows:

Break-even sales	$12,386	100.0%
Variable expense[1]	(8,711)	(70.33%)
Contribution margin	3,675	29.67%
Fixed expense	(3,675)	(29.67%)
Net Profit	-0-	0.00%

[1] Calculated by subtracting the CMR of 29.67% from 100 percent and multiplying by break-even sales.

Monthly break-even sales are calculated by dividing annual break-even sales by twelve:

$12,374 ÷ 12 = $1,031   monthly break-even sales

Allen has now learned some important aspects of the business that can help him plan for increased profitability. One is that he can now determine what sales level is required to obtain a desired profit. In order to produce a return on equity of 30 percent, net profit needs to be at least $458 (.30 x equity of $1,525—see 20X6 equity on the balance sheet on page 88).

We calculate the sales needed to achieve that profit using the following formula:

$$\frac{\text{Fixed expenses + desired profit}}{\text{Contribution margin ratio}} = \text{Required sales}$$

$$\frac{3,675 + 458}{.2967} = \text{Required sales of \$12,386}$$

If Allen knows that rent is going up $50 in 20X7, he can calculate the sales he would need to make a profit of $458 plus $50 in increased fixed expense by adding $50 to fixed expense as follows:

$$\frac{3,675 + 458 + 50}{.2967} = \text{Required sales of } \$14,098$$

Knowing how your expenses *behave*, either on a fixed or variable basis, allows you to calculate sales needed to either break even or generate a specific net profit. This is a valuable exercise to assist you in financial planning.

OPERATIONAL LEVERAGE

To some extent, you can change expenses from fixed to variable or vice versa. You can pay your sales people a salary (fixed expense), or you can pay them a commission (variable expense).

When we examined the balance sheet in chapter five, we looked at the debt-to-equity ratio which is a measure of the safety of the firm, and is also an indication of the amount of financial leverage that is being employed. Financial leverage refers to the amount of debt versus the amount of equity, and the higher the debt-to-equity, the higher the financial leverage.

High fixed expenses and low variable expenses is referred to as "operational leverage." High fixed expenses and low variable expenses produces a higher break-even sales level. That's the bad news. The good news is that once the break-even level has been exceeded, there are large potential profits. There is a little more bad news. If the sales level is below break-even, there are large potential losses.

In other words, high operational leverage produces higher business risk in the same manner as high financial leverage.

High operational leverage is illustrated by the following diagram.

HIGH FIXED EXPENSES, LOW VARIABLE EXPENSES

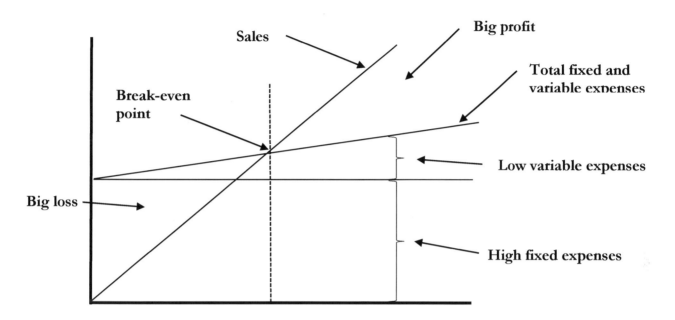

Large potential profit and large potential loss. Higher break-even point. More risk-More reward. High operational leverage.

If a firm combines high financial risk with high operational risk, the level of the overall risk of the company is increased significantly. An example of this would be starting up a manufacturing business (which typically is a business with high fixed and low variable expenses) with minimal capital (high debt-to-equity ratio and high financial leverage). This is an example of both high operational leverage and high financial leverage.

This is at least one reason why starting a manufacturing business is difficult and firms like Apple are started in someone's garage or basement, which takes minimal initial capital. This is opposed to starting a consulting firm (like I did) that needs a few computers and some used furniture (which is both cheap and abundantly available). Not a lot of initial capital is required and risk is further reduced by the low fixed and high variable expense pattern that is typical for a service firm like that.

Low fixed expenses reduce the break-even sales level. That's the good news, but the bad news is that it also reduces the amount of the potential profit. There is a little more good news. If sales are below the break-even level, there are smaller potential losses.

Low operational leverage is illustrated by the following diagram:

LOW FIXED EXPENSES, HIGH VARIABLE EXPENSES

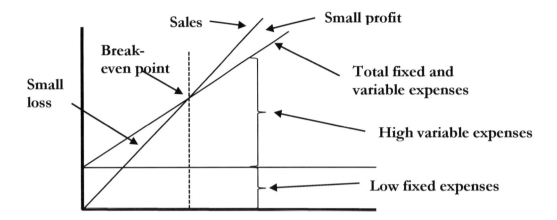

Small potential profit and small potential loss. Lower break-even point. Less risk-Less reward. Low operational leverage.

After studying the above two diagrams you now may think "OK I see what I want–low fixed expenses and low variable expenses." Nice try. You can have one or the other, but not both. Every time you convert a fixed expense, like sales salary, to a variable expense, like sales commission, you move from one to the other. You have reduced your break-even sales level and your risk of loss, and you have also reduced your potential profit once you exceed break-even sales. If your business is both cyclical and seasonal and is therefore inherently more risky, you might opt to convert as many fixed expenses as possible to variable. Study the options carefully and then strategize what will work best for your company.

Make sure you know your monthly break-even sales, and develop a business strategy that will meet or exceed that level monthly. Once you are profitable every month on a sustained basis you can think about converting selected variable expenses to fixed expenses to increase profitability.

STRATEGY FOR CORRECTING A LOSS

Let's assume that Durson Distributors experienced below break-even sales in 20X6 as follows:

Sales	$11,253
Variable expenses[1]	(7,914)
Contribution margin	3,339
Fixed expenses	(3,675)
Net profit	(336)

[1] Calculated by multiplying sales of $11,253 by 0.7033

The company has experienced a loss of $336, and the only way to correct this is to either increase sales to at least $12,374 or cut fixed expenses by at least that amount, assuming increasing sales is not an option. The expenses to cut are the fixed expenses, since cutting variable expenses would necessitate cutting sales (variable expenses are caused by and directly related to sales).

I hope that you can see that this expense behavior analysis is very valuable and informative. If we had not gone through this exercise for Durson Distributors, we would not know exactly how to correct the loss situation. Since we did, we know that Allen has to look carefully at his *fixed* expenses in order to see which ones can be reduced. He should act promptly and do this as soon as the loss is experienced, as discussed in chapter three.

Homework Assignment

Use the form on the next page to calculate break-even sales for Durson Distributors based upon the income statement forecast for 20X7 in chapter eleven. You should get $11,553 (assume all cost of goods sold are variable). Then take out the last fiscal year-end financial statement for your business and calculate your break-even sales, both annually and monthly.

The next chapter will discuss the capital budgeting process. Keep on paddling!

Break-even Worksheet

Year	20X6			20X7		
Sales	**13,100**	**Fixed**	**Variable**	**14,400**	**Fixed**	**Variable**
Cost of goods sold			8,725			
Advertising		180				
Bad debts			95			
Depreciation		126				
Equipment leases		88				
Insurance		201				
Legal and accounting		33				
Miscellaneous		81				
Office expense		71				
Payroll tax and benefits		412				
Rent		325				
Repairs and maintenance		31				
Salaries		1,480				
Sales commissions			393.			
Business tax and licenses		72				
Telephone and utilities		42				
Travel and entertainment		147				
Vehicle expense		201				
Interest expense[1]		175				
Total		**3,675**	**9,213**			

1. Exclude other income and other expenses from this analysis. Include only interest expense.

20X6

Sales of $13,100 - variable expense of $ 9,213 = contribution margin of $3,887.

Contribution margin ÷ sales = contribution margin ratio (CMR) of 29.67%.

Fixed expenses of $ 3,675 ÷ CMR of 29.67% = break-even sales of $12,386.

Break-even sales ÷ 12 = monthly break-even sales of $1,032.

20X7

Sales of $14,400 – variable expense of $_____ = contribution margin of

$_____

Contribution margin ÷ sales = contribution margin ratio (CMR) of _____%

Fixed expenses of $_____ ÷ CMR of _____% = Break-even sales of

$_____

Break-even sales ÷ 12 = monthly break-even sales of $_____

CHAPTER SEVENTEEN: CAPITAL BUDGETING

Fixed assets are expensive and involve a long-term commitment of funds. Most firms that are capital intensive have a capital expenditure budget for the year shortened to "cap-ex," based upon either formal or informal expectations for sales or the need to replace old equipment. However, in over thirty years I have never seen a business use any kind of a capital budgeting analysis.

The reasons for not using this tool are varied, but I believe it is primarily because business owners think about this simplistically. They ask and answer two questions; "Do I need the equipment?" and "Can I afford it?" If the answer is yes to both questions, the analysis is over.

Decisions to buy fixed assets are based upon experience and gut instincts, and most of the time they are probably correct. There is a tool, however, that can augment gut feelings with a little more formal analysis and it is called capital budgeting.

DEFINITION

Capital budgeting is the practice of allocating funds set aside for investment in fixed assets in the most effective manner. It takes into consideration the risks and possible returns of various potential investments. It is the process of determining whether or not an asset should be purchased based upon its estimated generated cash flows.

Example

The delivery van is getting on in years, and the transmission goes out. Should you fix it or buy a new one?

Capital budgeting is the answer to this and all other questions regarding the purchase of fixed assets, and this chapter describes the process that you should use.

Capital expenditures represent a significant amount of the company's financial resources and are a multi-year decision, so it is prudent to do an analysis to make sure that it is a sound financial decision.

STEPS IN THE CAPITAL BUDGETING PROCESS

1. Estimate the annual net cash income
2. Estimate salvage value
3. Establish the minimum acceptable return on the asset

ESTIMATE THE ANNUAL NET CASH INCOME.
Estimate the net cash income and/or decreased expenses each year for five years that will be generated by the equipment. Do not include depreciation, which is a non-cash expense, in this process, but you can include the tax savings of the depreciation into the cash income. It is the net cash income (cash income minus cash expense) that needs to be determined.

This may be estimated as a level amount, or it may vary from year to year. It is not possible to determine net cash income with precision for five years into the future, but this is not intended to be an exact science. Your best guess is sufficient, and it is wise to be conservative. If you have no idea how much a vehicle or piece of equipment will earn for your business over a period of years, then I would argue that you should not purchase it in the first place.

ESTIMATE THE SALVAGE VALUE.
Estimate the salvage value of the equipment at the end of five years and add that to the fifth-year cash income. This could be either be expressed as a percentage of the initial cost of the equipment, or you can use historical experience. Many items of used equipment have an established market value, and the value for a five-year-old truck can be compared to the original purchase price. Estimating zero salvage value for assets like computers would be the most conservative approach.

ESTABLISH A MINIMUM ACCEPTABLE RATE OF RETURN.
Establish a minimum acceptable rate of return required on the purchased asset. My opinion is that 15 percent should be a minimum for any industry, and a higher rate would be appropriate if the future profitability of the equipment is especially uncertain.

After these three steps have been completed, it is possible to calculate whether a particular fixed asset generates the minimum acceptable rate of return. This calculation involves calculating the net present value by comparing the present value of the future cash inflows to the present value of the cash outflow (the cost of the equipment plus shipping and set-up, if applicable).

For the purposes of this exercise, always assume that you are paying cash for the asset even if you expect to finance it with a long-term loan. The present value of the cash outflow is the initial cost of the equipment, plus shipping and setup, if required, less any cash received for an item that is being replaced.

Fortunately there is an Excel spreadsheet that comes with this book, so none of these calculations needs to be done manually. Download it at www.leadtosucceed.biz.

CASE STUDY: DURSON DISTRIBUTORS

The business has grown, and there is a need for an additional delivery van. A used truck has been located that is available for $40,000.

Step One:

Allen estimates that the truck will generate $11,000 in net cash income per year. (This amount is illustrative for purposes of this example and is not intended to reflect what a truck might generate in your business.)

Step Two:
Salvage value is estimated to be $7,000 at the end of five years.

Step Three:
Allen has decided that a minimum rate of return is 15%.

Calculations:

Year	Net Cash Flow		Present Value Factor	Equals	Present Value
0	($40,000)	x	1.0	=	($40,000)
1	$11,000	x	0.870	=	$9,570
2	$11,000	x	0.756	=	$8,316
3	$11,000	x	0.658	=	$7,238
4	$11,000	x	0.572	=	$6,292
5	$18,000[1]	x	0.497	=	$8,946
Net present value[2]					$362

[1].$11,000 plus $7,000 salvage value.
[2]. The present value of the cash inflow minus the present value of the cash outflow.

The present value factors used in this example are for a 15 percent return. We know that the return on this truck is in excess of 15 percent, because the net present value is a positive $362. If the net present value were zero, we would know that the return is exactly 15 percent, and if the net present value were negative, we would know that the return is less than 15 percent.

If the net present value is negative, the investment should be rejected since it does not produce the required minimum return.

Present value factors for various returns are:

year	15%	20%	25%	30%
0	1.0	1.0	1.0	1.0
1	0.870	0.833	0.800	0.769
2	0.756	0.694	0.640	0.592
3	0.658	0.579	0.512	0.455
4	0.572	0.482	0.410	0.350
5	0.497	0.402	0.328	0.269

SUMMARY

Acquisition of fixed assets requires committing a large portion of your company's resources over an extended number of years, and these types of decisions therefore deserve to be analyzed as carefully as possible. If your company has six potential capital investments in the coming year and only enough financial resources to fund five of them, then you can calculate the estimated net present value of all six and pick the five highest.

The most difficult part of this exercise is certainly not the actual calculations. Those are simple arithmetic, and there is software available with this book to do it for you (find it at www.leadtosucceed.biz). The more challenging aspect of the exercise is forecasting the cash returns for five years with any degree of certainty. Like any forecasting exercise, this is not meant to be precise, but if you have no idea how much a piece of equipment might generate in income you should not buy it. This is an important economic decision that should not be based totally on gut instincts.

Your money is not unlimited, so it should be invested as carefully and as wisely as possible. Go through this exercise even if you are not completely sure how or why it works. Give it your best shot. This analysis is better than nothing, and you will gain greater understanding each time you do it.

Use this tool, and become one of the first in the history of your industry to do so!

Homework Assignment

Pick an investment that you have made in the past and see if you can determine the return on investment that it is generating for you based upon what it is earning in cash inflow.

The next chapter will describe some of the unique aspects of leading a service business. Keep on paddling!

CHAPTER EIGHTEEN: THE SERVICE BUSINESS

CEOs of service businesses face a little bit different set of challenges.

Service businesses do not have cost of goods sold because they sell services and not goods. Because of this, owners of these businesses may feel that they do not have a gross profit. They simply have revenue and expenses, resulting in a net profit. Consulting firms, law firms, and restaurants all may believe this to be true and therefore do not have an income statement that reflects a gross profit. This is a huge mistake and hampers their ability to measure and maximize profitability all three levels that have been discussed previously.

If you own a service business and do not reflect a gross profit on your income statement you should work with your accountant or bookkeeper to change the income statement format so that your expenses are separated into direct and indirect categories. Direct expenses are those that are directly related to generating revenue, and indirect expenses are all others.

For a law firm, as an example, compensation for lawyers and para-legal assistants would be direct expenses; and the receptionist, office manager, rent, utilities, and accounting department would be indirect expenses. Not very many law firms reflect a gross profit on their income statement because they either don't feel it is applicable to them or they don't see any advantage in doing so. This is a mistake. The gross profit and gross profit margin are crucial to every business, and should be measured and analyzed on a regular basis.

Industry ratio averages are available for most service businesses, but the average gross profit margin is rarely available due to the lack of gross profit information provided by reporting firms. If this is the case for your business, it is incumbent upon you to measure your gross profit margin on a regular basis and then set your own standard as a goal since industry information does not exist. Then calculate this ratio regularly to ensure that you are attaining your goal.

If inventory is not a significant asset of your business then the inventory days ratio does not need to be calculated. If you are primarily a cash business then the days sales outstanding ratio does not need to be calculated. All of the other ratios apply equally to a service business and should be calculated and monitored on a regular basis.

Some service businesses can grow faster due to the fact that they are not capital intensive (i.e. need a lot of assets). As sales go up, assets go up and cash flow goes down, but if there aren't that many assets required in the business, growth is easier from a cash flow standpoint. The limiting factor for growth is that often the primary assets are human, and it is not that easy to double the staff if revenue doubles. Skilled and trained engineering consultants are not always readily available, as an example.

Service business owners who are reading this book should be mindful that despite the fact that they do not make or sell a product, all of the tenets discussed in this book apply to them just as much as any other type of business.

If you have a contracting business you have accounts on your balance sheet that are not typical of most business types. Examples are *costs and estimated earnings in excess of billings on uncompleted contracts* that is a current asset, and *billings in excess of costs and estimated earnings on uncompleted contracts* that is a current liability. Accounting systems for contractors are more complicated than most businesses due to the need to estimate the completion of a contract and the resulting revenue and expenses.

A detailed explanation of contractor accounting is beyond the scope of this book but my advice is to make sure you thoroughly understand all of the concepts and terms used and how they impact the principles of financial analysis as outlined in this book. Study all of that and make sure you discuss this in depth with your CPA. You have plenty else to do but you need to fully understand what all of that means from a financial and cash flow standpoint.

The next chapter will describe how to deal with your banker and always get the loans you ask for. Keep on paddling!

CHAPTER NINETEEN: DEALING WITH YOUR BANKER

You may feel that the only time you can get a loan from a bank is when you don't need it, or that the only one who has not been turned down by a bank is one who has never applied.

Bankers *can* seem to be difficult. They ask a lot of questions. Where is your business going? How will you get there? What does your projected cash flow look like? What are your anticipated borrowing requirements, and how do you expect to repay? What is your financial knowledge and expertise? By the time you get through with this third degree, you're convinced that bankers are placed on earth primarily to make your life more complicated and difficult.

Applying the concepts presented in this book, however, will take your relationship to new heights and ensure that your banker becomes an integral member of your team.

ESTABLISH A RELATIONSHIP

Good communication about the financial condition of your business is paramount in establishing a successful relationship with your banker, and the principles of financial management described in this book are the keys to good communication. When you complete your historical analysis and financial projections, you gain credibility as someone who actually has a grasp of the business from a financial standpoint. You will stand out in the top 1 or 2 percent of the bank's customers who provide such information. As your banker gains confidence in your ability to manage your business on a sound financial basis, you will be working in harmony for the financial success of your business.

Of course it's not true that the only time you can get a loan from a bank is when you don't need it. Making loans is how the bank makes money, and it is always looking to make loans to good, profitable, well-run businesses. After reading and applying the principles of this book, your business will be one of those.

DEBT VS. EQUITY

The two sources that are available to provide funds for your business are debt (money from banks, finance companies, trade creditors, and other lenders), and equity (money from owners). The general rule for financing a business is *equity first, debt second*. A strong equity base allows you to work from a position of strength when you seek debt. With a low debt-to-equity ratio, you will be less risky, and debt will therefore be less expensive (in the form of lower interest rates). Your debt-to-equity ratio is likely to be high in the wonder and blunder phases of business, and it will, therefore, be more difficult to obtain bank financing.

The reverse is also true. If you seek debt first and reach or exceed your borrowing limits and then seek equity capital out of desperation, you will have to give up much more in the way of ownership in order to raise the needed capital. Your company will be risky, and equity capital will be both difficult and expensive to obtain.

EQUITY FINANCING

Equity first, debt second. It sounds simple enough, but it may not always be possible. Where will you get equity capital? A full discussion of angel financing, venture capital, or public offerings is beyond the scope of this book; however, only a small minority of businesses will qualify for any of that. You are most likely limited to either raising money yourself (available savings, sale or mortgage of your home, etc.) or hitting up friends and relatives.

If you have already put all your available funds into the business, then your options are limited to friends and relatives. In fact, your options are probably limited to *older* friends and relatives who have lived long enough to accumulate the money needed to help you. Putting money in your business, however, may not be exactly where they ought to invest funds set aside for retirement. In any case I believe that you should think about borrowing from friends or relatives very carefully. Initial plans are laced heavily with supreme optimism and are seldom achieved. Because of this, there is a strong likelihood that relationships may be severely damaged, maybe irreparably. You need to think about whether borrowing to start a business is worth risking that. Fully documented loan agreements help in reducing legal arguments at a later time.

While equity financing is tough, a minimum amount needs to be provided to ensure continued financial viability. Financial projections, as discussed in chapters eleven through thirteen, can indicate how much capital will likely be required. Update this frequently, as additional information regarding actual performance is available. Remember the rule of thumb that it always takes twice as long and twice as much as initially planned.

If you intend to raise equity capital from the general public, seek the advice of qualified lawyers, accountants, and business valuation experts who are experienced in this type of transaction. The legal requirements are complicated, and this is *not* a do-it-yourself project.

If you are seeking equity capital, prepare a detailed business and financial plan, be aware of liabilities to which you may be exposed, and make sure you get proper legal assistance.

DEBT FINANCING

The discussion concerning debt financing in the rest of this chapter will assume that a commercial bank is the source of the funds. The general principles also apply to other sources of debt, such as business factors, finance or leasing companies, savings and loans, insurance companies, and the government.

If traditional bank financing is not available to you, research other available publications for more detailed information. The Small Business Association has an extensive list of publications that can provide information about financing sources and available programs.

STRUCTURING DEBT

Your business is likely to require three main categories of debt.

1. Short-term debt
2. Intermediate-term debt
3. Long-term debt

All your loans will fall into one of these categories, and it's important that you understand the type of debt you are requesting from the bank. This involves answering the following questions:

1. How much are you going to need?
2. How long will you need it?
3. How do you expect to be able to pay it back?

You'd be amazed at the number of business owners who cannot answer these questions with any degree of accuracy or sophistication when they request a loan from a bank. They rely instead on instincts and a seat-of-the-pants approach to financing their business. Then, when they do not get a warm reception at the bank, they complain that bankers are not really there to help. If they never read a book like this one, these business owners often become part of the large percentage of businesses that don't survive.

SHORT-TERM DEBT

Short-term bank debt is that which is due within one year. It can take the form of a fixed maturity loan, such as 90 or 120 days, or it can be structured in the form of a line of credit that is negotiated at the beginning of the year and made available as needed during the year. It is used to finance seasonal cash flow needs, such as an increase in accounts receivable, paying wages, and other expenses. Interest is usually floating, but it might be set for the year. The expectation is that the line of credit will start out at zero at the beginning of the year, rise to some predicted level during the busy season, and fall to zero at or before the end of the year.

Collateral for a line of credit is usually accounts receivables, and banks will generally provide up to 75 percent of your accounts receivable less than ninety days old.

INTERMEDIATE-TERM DEBT

Intermediate-term bank debt is the amount of your line of credit, if any, that remains unpaid at the end of the year. Bankers may tolerate this, but it is not something they like to do. It's an indication that your working capital and cash flow are not adequate to fund your business. By utilizing the analysis and forecasting techniques in this book, you can determine approximately when and how this situation will be corrected. The goal should be to pay off your line of credit by the end of the year and not have any intermediate-term bank debt.

LONG-TERM DEBT

Long-term debt is used for the purchase of fixed assets. The amount of the loan is limited to a percentage of the cost or value of the asset. The term is usually three to five years, depending on the asset. Land and buildings can typically be financed for up to twenty years, but it's not a good idea from a tax standpoint to own these inside your company (talk to your CPA further about this if you have not done so already).

Regular payments are required, and interest can be either fixed or floating. Collateral consists of the asset purchased, and sometimes all of the other equipment as well.

Even though it is straightforward, banks are sometimes not so eager to make long-term loans. The reason is that the banker has to make a determination regarding your ability to make payments several years into the future, and this presents a higher degree of uncertainty and risk. For this reason, long-term loans are usually only available to well-established businesses that have a good payment record and a demonstrated track record of profitability.

Leasing fixed assets is an alternative to buying, and sometimes the credit requirements are less strict for this type of transaction. Ask your CPA for help and advice, as structuring a lease is a complex exercise from a tax standpoint.

LOAN AGREEMENT

Most loans are covered by a loan agreement, and you can expect to negotiate loan covenants as part of this agreement. Covenants (minimum or maximum levels for various ratios) may take the form of a minimum current ratio, a maximum debt-to-equity ratio, a minimum interest coverage ratio, or a minimum dollar amount of working capital or equity. There also may be restrictions on owner's compensation, dividends, and repayment of shareholder loans.

These covenants are negotiable, and you should be cautious about agreeing to any that you are not confident you can achieve. Failure to comply with any of the loan covenants allows the bank to demand immediate repayment of the balance. The bank may temporarily waive the covenant, but you don't want to count on this. If you do not understand any of the covenants proposed by the bank, be sure to keep asking until you do.

You should also be cautious about tying up all your assets for a particular loan, thereby restricting your ability to finance your business in the future. Including accounts receivable as collateral for an equipment loan, as an example, makes it difficult or impossible to obtain a line of credit because your accounts receivable are securing other debt. You should agree to this only as a last resort.

INTEREST RATES

How, you ask, does the bank determine your interest rate? On some sort of arbitrary and capricious basis?

The factors that determine the interest rate that you will pay at the bank are as follows:

1. The risk level of your business.

2. The cost of funds to the bank (interest on certificates of deposit, savings accounts, etc.).
3. The term of the loan (longer-term loans are usually riskier and therefore have a higher interest rate).
4. The amount of the loan (smaller loans cost as much to make as bigger loans and therefore may have a higher interest rate).
5. The collateral (some forms of collateral are more difficult and therefore more costly to administer).
6. The average balances that you maintain in your checking account (the more you maintain, the lower your rate).
7. The supply and demand for loanable funds.
8. The bank's competition.

All of the above are going to determine your interest rate, but you should be aware that interest rates are usually negotiable. Most lending officers have some discretion about the rates that they can charge, and you should speak up if you feel yours is too high.

If you determine that a competing bank is willing to offer the same type of loan at a lower interest rate, then go back to your bank with this information. The bank can either match the competition or risk losing your business. Don't be tempted to switch banks on a frequent basis to get a somewhat-lower interest rate. This won't build loyalty between you and the bank and may eventually hinder your ability to obtain bank loans.

THE FIVE CS OF CREDIT

Bankers tend to look at a loan request within the context of the five Cs of credit. In order of importance they are:

1. Character
2. Capacity
3. Capital
4. Collateral
5. Conditions

CHARACTER
Bankers want to look you in the eye and see an honest, ethical person. They do not want to work with people of marginal character, no matter how strong the deal. It is the most important criterion they have, and they will check you out as thoroughly as possible to see if your word is good.

CAPACITY
Once you pass the character test, you need to demonstrate that you have the capacity to repay the loan. This is done by establishing a track record and by presenting well-thought-out projections that indicate repayment is probable.

CAPITAL

Every business needs a sufficient base of capital (equity) in order to qualify for bank loans. The *amount* of required capital is a subjective judgment, but it will usually be tied to your debt-to-equity ratio, as discussed in chapter five. If your ratio is high, as it might be in the wonder or blunder phases of business, this will make obtaining bank loans more difficult, if not impossible. Before asking for a loan, put yourself in your banker's shoes, and ask yourself if you would loan money to a high-risk start-up business lacking a strong balance sheet and a track record of stable profitability.

COLLATERAL

There is an unwritten rule in banking that loans should not be granted solely on the basis of available collateral, because collateral does not make a bad loan good. It is still a bad loan. In other words, there should be every indication that the collateral will never be required and that it is only taken to allow the bank to recover its funds in the case of some unforeseen event. There are asset-based lenders who make loans based solely on collateral, but they are not banks.

Bankers always ask for collateral, and they always utilize accounts receivable, but it is only fourth in the order of importance as to whether or not they make a loan.

Strong, well-run, and financially stable businesses with good track records are sometimes able to borrow on an unsecured basis, but not many.

CONDITIONS

The last *C* refers to those conditions that are largely outside of your control—the economy, and the industry. Difficult times will negatively impacted the willingness of banks to provide loans.

PERSONAL GUARANTEES

As you have probably already discovered, bankers look for not one (cash flow), not two (collateral), but *three* sources of repayment. The third source is your personal guarantee.

The standard assumption is that bankers never make a loan to a closely held business without the personal guarantees of the owners. This is not always true. Some businesses are strong enough to stand on their own and do not require the personal guarantee of the owner. If you feel that you are in this elite group, then speak up. Make your case. Let the banker tell you why you must personally guarantee the debt.

The bank is unlikely to initiate the subject of dropping your personal guarantee once you have one in place. If the bank already has your guarantee, then it will want to keep it. If you want to change this situation, it is up to you to bring it up. If you are making a loan request for the first time, then state at the outset that you are not expecting to guarantee the loan. Test the waters. See what they say. Such a proclamation may be enough to avoid this requirement.

In the final analysis, don't be overly reluctant to personally guarantee a loan. This may indicate to the bank that you don't have confidence in the ability of the business to repay the loan. Personal liability is something that you obviously want to avoid, but not at the expense of restricting your borrowing ability. In any case, it's OK to have this discussion with the bank.

RULES OF BEHAVIOR

There are a few rules of behavior that you should follow in building a relationship with your banker.

RULE NUMBER ONE—WORK ON ESTABLISHING A GOOD RELATIONSHIP
Invite your banker to functions of a social, non-business nature, such as out on your boat (that you acquired in the thunder phase of business), to a football game, or to the theater. Get to know each other on more than a business basis in order to deepen your relationship.

Absolutely nothing will cement your relationship like getting your banker additional business. Refer prospective customers.

Make sure your banker visits your business. Get your banker on your turf to meet your key people.

Get to know your banker's boss, and maybe even the boss's boss. This ensures some degree of continuity when, or if, the lending officer handling your account changes.

RULE NUMBER TWO—ALWAYS BE PREPARED
Put yourself in your banker's place. What information would you want? What questions would you have? Anticipate these in advance, and be prepared with answers. Never assume that your banker understands your business; take the time to describe it thoroughly.

Overkill with information. More is better. It will make a good first impression.

RULE NUMBER THREE—ALWAYS KEEP YOUR BANKER INFORMED
Provide accurate and timely information about your business. Send the bank quarterly financial statements at least, with appropriate comments and explanations. You and perhaps your CFO should meet with the bank two to three times per year or more.

Tell it all—the good and the bad. The bank will find out anyway, and trying to hide something will hurt your credibility and your relationship.

RULE NUMBER FOUR—NEVER BLUFF
If you don't know the answer to a question, say so. If you don't understand something, say so. Bankers don't mean to be intimidating, and they welcome any questions you might have. Don't worry about appearing to be stupid when you ask questions. Bankers have their own jargon, just as you do in your business, and you cannot be expected to be familiar with all of the banking terms. Besides, some banks may define them differently than others. Make sure you really understand what they are saying.

RULE NUMBER FIVE—NEVER ASSUME ANYTHING

Bankers occasionally say things like, "That looks like something we could do," but that is not meant as a commitment to make a loan. People hear what they want to hear. Make sure you understand the difference between an offhand comment and a commitment. Commitments are made in writing.

Bankers sometimes tell you bad news in a nice way. When they say that they have determined you to be a *special credit*, as an example, this doesn't mean they really like you. It means you are in the loans-that-need-special-attention category for some reason, and you may be one step away from getting booted out of the bank.

RULE NUMBER SIX—NEVER, UNDER ANY CIRCUMSTANCES, SURPRISE YOUR BANKER

Bankers, like most people, do not like surprises.

There is a strong temptation to tell your bankers only what they want to hear or specifically ask about. When they find out the rest of the story, they are surprised. Then they are upset. This is seldom good.

OUTLINE OF BANK PRESENTATION

I. Proposal
- A. Durson Distributors is seeking the following bank accommodations:
  - 1. $750,000 revolving line of credit utilizing accounts receivable as collateral.
  - 2. $1,000,000 equipment term loan line of credit secured by equipment.
- B. Proceeds will be used for seasonal cash flow needs and purchase of equipment.

II. Overview
- A. Description of the business
  - Form of business (C Corp, S Corp, or LLC)
  - Owners
  - Date started
  - Locations
  - Board of directors
  - Vision statement
  - Mission statement
  - Core values
- B. Key officers and management
  - Position
  - Experience
  - Tenure
  - Age
- C. Organization chart reflecting all key positions and reporting relationships
- D. Key advisors: legal, accounting, insurance, etc.
- E. Descriptions of insurance coverage

III. Description of market and products
- A. Business lines as percentage of sales
- B. Major customers

    C. Market size
    D. Market share
    E. Primary competition
    F. Description of sales and marketing strategy
IV. Description of facilities
    Size, location, condition, capacity, etc.
V. Financial
    A. Three years of income statements
    B. Three years of balance sheets
    C. Three years of cash flow
    D. Three years of financial ratios with management comments
    E. Projected income statement, balance sheet, statement of cash flow, and ratios
    F. Copy of most recent tax return
    G. Comments on financial condition and forecast
VI. Strategic Goals and Objectives for the year
Appendixes
    1. Owner resumes
    2. References
    3. Shareholder agreement, if any
    4. Equipment list – model, year, cost, estimated value
    5. List of existing leases/contracts
    6. By-laws and articles of incorporation

SUMMARY

Few things are more crucial to your long-term success than financing your business properly and professionally. Analyze your debt requirements thoroughly, and communicate this information clearly and concisely to your banker.

Make sure you are well prepared when you make a presentation to the bank. Use the bank-presentation outline in this chapter as a guide of what should be included.

Your loans or line of credit at the bank are usually governed by a loan agreement that stipulates terms, interest rates, and covenants that restrict your ability to pay dividends and owner's salary or repay shareholder loans. Covenants may consist of a minimum current ratio, a minimum amount of working capital (current assets minus current liabilities), a maximum debt-to-equity ratio, or a minimum debt-coverage or interest-coverage ratio. Make sure you understand what these covenants are and how they are calculated.

There are six important rules to follow in your dealings with your banker:

    1. Establish a good personal relationship.
    2. Be prepared.
    3. Keep your banker informed.
    4. Never bluff.
    5. Never assume.
    6. Never surprise.

Take great pains to educate your banker about your business, and answer any questions. Make sure everyone agrees about what is expected. Get it in writing. When problems arise, people tend to have selective memories about what was said. If you follow these rules of behavior with those who lend you money, your life will be a lot easier, and your reputation as a good businessperson will be greatly enhanced at the bank.

The final chapter will provide you with some helpful hints about how to work effectively with your CPA. Keep on paddling!

CHAPTER TWENTY: DEALING WITH YOUR CPA

Always surround yourself with knowledgeable advisors. Selecting the right CPA, who is knowledgeable in business accounting, may be one of the most important business decisions you will make. Don't hesitate to ask prospective CPAs for references and experience with companies in your industry.

TRADITIONAL VERSUS VALUE-ADDED SERVICE

Technical accounting knowledge is only one aspect of an effective CPA. Traditionally, CPAs have acted as historians by providing financial information in the form of financial statements or tax returns. They may not have been concerned about whether you understood, or could adequately interpret, the information they provided. If your business was experiencing difficulties, financial or otherwise, they likely would not comment on that.

Today, well-run CPA firms have a much broader perception of their roles in your business. They take a proactive approach to such things as interpretation of your financial ratios and IRS regulations that may affect you. They examine and assist you with management information systems in your business and ownership-succession planning issues. In other words, the "green eyeshade number crunchers" of the past have been replaced by a new breed of CPAs who focus on helping businesses interpret and monitor financial information in a proactive way. This has changed the role of the CPA from just a historian to a trusted financial and business advisor, and that is what you should expect from your CPA.

Since the late 1980s, the accounting profession has grown more complex, and some firms have not kept up with changes in tax laws, financial reporting, and computerization. In the past, it was easier to be a generalist, but in today's environment, this is much more difficult.

If you are considering dealing with a large international firm, make sure that they have a division that is experienced in serving small and medium-sized businesses, and be sure to get references from firms that you interview.

ACCOUNTING SYSTEMS

The center of an accounting system is the general ledger (GL). Other components include accounts receivable (AR), accounts payable (AP), payroll, fixed assets, orders and billing, inventory, etc. The accounting system can be manual or computerized or a combination of both.

Many companies think that by virtue of having an expensive computer system, they have a good accounting system. Unfortunately, this is not always true. The accounting system is where financial transactions are recorded, monitored, and controlled. The computer may be the hub of the accounting system, but it is not responsible for making sure the entered transactions are accurate, properly controlled, and monitored. A poorly designed and monitored accounting system may allow fraud or unintentional errors to go undetected for years, and the loss to your business can be substantial before it is discovered.

Who is responsible for making sure your accounting system is operating properly? The CPA? Your controller or CFO? The ultimate answer to this question is that you and your CPA must make sure that any weaknesses are corrected in your business. Your CPA should be able to help you design and monitor your accounting system and its controls in a cost-effective way.

MONITORING THE SYSTEMS

Many businesses have complex accounting systems that are difficult to review properly, and some CPAs do not spend sufficient time testing underlying accounting systems, making sure that sales and expenses are properly captured and recorded in the correct time period. For most businesses, system testing is important, and owners should ask for a management letter from their CPA regarding any ideas or suggestions they might have.

Your CPA should play an important part in providing you with assurance that your business's systems are operating in an appropriate manner, with adequate built-in controls. If you receive a reviewed or audited financial statement, make sure that you request a management letter, which discusses your accounting and management systems and controls. If you contract for a reviewed statement instead of an audited statement, your CPA will probably not be paying as much attention to your accounting system and controls unless you specifically ask that this be done.

LEVELS OF FINANCIAL STATEMENTS

COMPILED FINANCIAL STATEMENTS

The simplest form of financial statements that your CPA might provide you is called a *compiled* statement. These statements consist of placing the numbers that you generate internally on the letterhead of the accounting firm. In the process, the accountant looks at the statements and makes adjusting entries related to obvious errors.

Compiled financial statements are OK for most small firms but are typically not given too much credence by lenders for larger firms that require substantial financing.

REVIEWED FINANCIAL STATEMENTS

In reviewed financial statements, the CPA makes general inquiries of management and performs some analytical procedures. Inquiries are made concerning key financial information. Analytical review procedures include a review of financial ratios, which are used to support the assertions of management and corroborate the answers to inquiries.

Although reviewed financial statements are substantially less in scope than an audit, they are well-received by the financial community for several reasons, including:

1. Reviewed statements holds the CPA to a higher level of responsibility than compiled statements.
2. The cost of a reviewed statement is much less than an audit.
3. The financial statements and related notes are more reliable.

4. Reviewed financial statements provide a good starting point for trend and cash flow analysis.
5. It shows a commitment by the owners to hold their organizations to higher standards of reporting.

Reviewed financial statements can also serve as an annual checkup of your accounting department. Through the inquiry process, your CPA may be able to determine if accounts have been reconciled and whether your accounting department is operating efficiently.

A reviewed statement can be a good start in helping a CPA understand your accounting systems. However, many CPAs do not extend their work beyond the required inquiries and analytical procedures. Make sure you ask about your CPA's procedures regarding your accounting system, and whether there are any recommendations as a result of their observations.

For many smaller firms, compiled financial statements are satisfactory, but for larger and more complex firms that generate several million in sales, a reviewed financial statement will be a more dependable document and will likely be required by the bank.

AUDITED FINANCIAL STATEMENTS

In an audit, the CPA performs specific audit procedures to determine whether or not your financial statements are in accordance with generally accepted accounting procedures (GAAP). The results of the audit are expressed in a letter of opinion that is issued by the CPA as a cover letter to the financial statements. An audit is in-depth and thus more expensive than a review or compilation. It includes detailed tests of account balances, testing of internal control procedures, and analytical review procedures designed to help provide the CPA with the necessary assurances to express an opinion, with the added benefit of helping the CPA understand your business.

Most businesses do not need audited financial statements, but some larger businesses must have an audit to satisfy banking requirements or shareholders not active in the business. Because of the expense involved, make sure you understand the reason for an audit. At a cost of two to three times that of a review, you should challenge the need for an audit.

In theory, the results presented in your financial statements, whether compiled, reviewed, or audited, should be the same. These statements should all conform to generally accepted accounting principles and include, in addition to the balance sheet and income statement, a statement of cash flow, retained earnings, and related notes.

The major differences between the various types of CPA-prepared financial statements are the accountant's opinion letter, the degree of verification of the information, the extensiveness of notes, and the cost.

Think about the level of financial statements that you need in your business, and discuss this with your CPA.

TAX ISSUES

Taxation of businesses is complex and challenging. Your CPA needs to have adequate training and knowledge of your industry.

Your CPA should advise you as to whether you should elect *S* corporation status or remain a *C* corporation. If you are a *C* corporation and have never discussed this with your CPA, make sure you bring it up because there may be considerable benefits to you in electing *S* corporation status.

If you are planning to sell your business, talk to your CPA *well in advance* about the tax issues you will face in this process.

Tax-planning discussions need to occur well before year-end. Planning is the most important part of reducing taxes, and proper tax planning can minimize the amount of tax that you have to pay. Your CPA should be proactive in this process. Your year-end income tax liability should not be a surprise; it should be the by-product of proper advanced planning.

RULES FOR WORKING WITH YOUR CPA

Like working with your banker, there are rules of behavior that you should follow when working with your CPA.

RULE NUMBER ONE—GET YOUR CPA INVOLVED

Your CPA should be an integral member of your advisory team who will help you with a variety of issues, from establishing proper accounting systems to helping you plan for the long-term future of your business.

RULE NUMBER TWO—ASK A LOT OF QUESTIONS

CPAs have generic terms that are common to their profession. Make sure that you ask questions every time they use a term you don't understand. If you don't understand the first answer, keep asking until you do. Communication is the key to obtaining satisfactory service from your CPA and you should not hesitate to be proactive in this area.

Ask your CPA questions such as:

1. How am I doing, in your opinion?
2. How can I improve my accounting system?
3. What suggestions do you have for me to improve my profitability?
4. What are your thoughts about our industry and the economy for the coming year?
5. What should I be doing in the way of estate planning?
6. Do I have enough life insurance?
7. How can you help me interpret my financial performance and prepare a financial plan for next year?
8. Does my accounting staff appear to have a good understanding and competence in their respective roles?

If you get a lot of blank stares or vague answers, consider changing accountants.

RULE NUMBER THREE—TALK REGULARLY

Be proactive and talk to your accountant at least once a quarter. Never assume that your employees know all the answers to questions you might have or are performing their jobs correctly. Checking and verifying your records and procedures on a regular basis will save you much more money than it ever costs you in accounting fees.

RULE NUMBER FOUR—DON'T PROCRASTINATE

Every time you call your CPA, the meter is running, and so there is a natural tendency to put it off. Besides, you are busy running your business and responding to the multitude of questions and problems that you face on a daily basis. For the same reason it is not a good idea to put off calling your doctor when you have chest pains, it is not a good idea to put off communicating with your CPA. CPAs can help you solve little problems before they become big ones.

RULE NUMBER FIVE—DON'T PUT UP WITH POOR SERVICE

Sometimes CPA firms become complacent about long-time clients. The most responsive service is often oriented toward the newest clients. Make sure that this doesn't happen to you and that you get what you are paying for. If you aren't receiving good service, let your CPA firm know that you're putting your job out for bids. This will send the message that you expect them to be competitive and responsive, *or else*. I realize that you may be loyal or close friends with your CPA, but an experienced, qualified, involved, and responsive CPA firm is an integral part of your overall success, and you need to manage this relationship accordingly.

SUMMARY

The need for an outside CPA who understands your business is more important than ever, and your CPA should be able to assist you in navigating the complexities of today's business and tax environments. You are ultimately responsible for managing the relationship with your CPA. Make sure that the CPA firm you select is knowledgeable and experienced in your business and has the depth to provide you with financial and tax services. Ask for references. Request and expect timely service.

You and your controller should meet with your CPA three to four times a year to discuss business in general and any questions or concerns you might have, especially regarding tax planning. The CPA should prepare annual tax returns and financial statements and also assist you with things like depreciation schedules, tax planning management systems and controls, and succession planning.

If you process payroll internally without using the services of an outside third-party firm, it is very important that you have your CPA review your procedures. You are required to file several quarterly tax returns as well as annual filings, and it is important that you pay deposits for payroll taxes for both your firm and your employees when they are due. Failure to comply with these requirements can result in substantial fines and penalties and your CPA is the one to help insure that you are in compliance in this area.

Your CPA is the best person, in addition to your banker, to help you understand, utilize, and implement the contents of this book, and should therefore be an important member of your advisory team.

CONCLUSION

This is a book about how to run a successful business. Success in your business cannot be achieved by one person however; it is a team effort, and effective leaders understand this. They surround themselves with smart, well-trained people who manage the key areas of their business. They delegate duties and responsibilities to their key managers and hold them accountable for results. Effective leaders hire people who are smarter than they are and who want to be part of a winning team. They do not settle for mediocrity. Make sure your under-performing employees understand what is required to maintain their employment.

Leading a successful business is a lifetime learning proposition, and it is helpful to observe others in a leadership capacity and determine what they do well and what they do not do as well. You can do this within your industry as you meet and observe other owners, and you can also do this by observing leaders of public companies.

A great example of a leader to pattern yourself after is Alan Mulally, CEO of Ford Motor Company. Showing great courage, he left a good job at the Boeing Company, where he was credited with heroic-like performance, and took the reins of a virtually bankrupt Ford Motor Company. He built a team of executives who were successful in saving the company and preserved hundreds of thousands of jobs in the process. Read the book on how he did it (refer to the bibliography), and then be just like Alan.

A leader you might not want to emulate is Steve Jobs, former CEO of Apple (see the bibliography for a book about him). Steve had great vision, but by all other accounts, he was not a very nice or compassionate person. He was arrogant, rude, and mean to those around him. He was not an effective leader and was dismissed as the CEO of Apple on more than one occasion because of that.

Watch and learn from others. Ask your direct reports how you are doing by using the upstream evaluation in appendix II. Ask your employees if they enjoy working at your company by using the employee satisfaction index in appendix I. Ensure your company will survive after you are gone by doing your succession planning as outlined in appendix IV. Cultivate a group of CEOs that you like and respect and ask them for advice and counsel.

Keep this book close by, and occasionally re-read a chapter. Give a copy of this book to all the members of your leadership team, and review parts of it on a regular basis. Better yet, have your key people teach parts of it in your monthly management meetings. People learn what they teach, and this information needs to be reviewed regularly until it becomes second nature, or it will be lost. Nothing is more powerful than a leadership team that understands these concepts and are pulling in the same harness and working together to make it happen.

Success is not pre-destined. It takes hard work. Eventually good leadership and financial understanding will become part of the culture and fabric of your company, and your employees will understand how they can help you achieve success and perpetual profitability. They will be winners who will hire winners and will want to play on a winning team.

So here we are, a little further along on our journey in the canoe. You are stronger for having paddled this far, but for you and me to be an effective team, you must keep working. Keep paddling. Otherwise we will go around in circles and not get very far.

And no, we are not there yet. So keep on paddling!

David A. Duryee
2015

APPENDIX I

EMPLOYEE SATISFACTION INDEX

Date: _____
Strictly Confidential

Poor 1—Excellent 10

Score

1. I have good access to my boss/supervisor.   _____

2. I feel that my boss adequately communicates with me.   _____

3. I feel like my opinions/feelings are important.   _____

4. I understand the goals of my department and the company.   _____

5. I receive sufficient training/information to do my job.   _____

6. I understand my career path.   _____

7. I have adequate physical space.   _____

8. I have adequate work equipment.   _____

9. I feel my compensation is fair and competitive.   _____

10. Overall I enjoy working here.   _____

Total Score   _____

Comments:

_____

_____

_____

APPENDIX II

UPSTREAM EVALUATION

Confidential

Evaluation of _____   Date_____

1. Provides effective and consistent leadership to the company.

Consistently   Usually   Sometimes   Never   Not Rated
Comments:

2. Demonstrates a passion for excellence.

Consistently   Usually   Sometimes   Never   Not Rated
Comments:

3. Requires noticeably superior service to customers.

Consistently   Usually   Sometimes   Never   Not Rated
Comments:

4. Sets clear goals and objectives for subordinates.

Consistently   Usually   Sometimes   Never   Not Rated
Comments:

5. Effectively delegates work, responsibility, and authority.

Consistently   Usually   Sometimes   Never   Not Rated
Comments:

6. Includes me in major decisions that affect me.

Consistently   Usually   Sometimes   Never   Not Rated
Comments:

7. Helps me to develop my skills by providing opportunities for growth and challenge.

Consistently   Usually   Sometimes   Never   Not Rated
Comments:

8. Conducts timely and constructive reviews of my performance.

Consistently   Usually   Sometimes   Never   Not Rated
Comments:

9. Makes time for me when I have suggestions, questions, or problems.

Consistently   Usually   Sometimes   Never   Not Rated
Comments:

10. Listens attentively and cares about my opinions and thoughts.

Consistently   Usually   Sometimes   Never   Not Rated
Comments:

11. Gives me recognition for my contributions and efforts to help the company.

Consistently   Usually   Sometimes   Never   Not Rated
Comments:

12. Knows and understands the core values of the company and strives to emulate them.

Consistently   Usually   Sometimes   Never   Not Rated
Comments:

13. Treats people with respect.

Consistently   Usually   Sometimes   Never   Not Rated
Comments:

14. Maintains a consistently high moral and ethical standard in his or her actions.

Consistently   Usually   Sometimes   Never   Not Rated
Comments:

15. What do you like most about this individual?

16. What suggestions would you have that would improve your working relationship?

APPENDIX III

BUSINESS REVIEW

This appendix contains questions that you and your key management team should carefully and accurately answer about the current state of your business. The list of questions is comprehensive and covers the following areas:

<u>Category</u>
1. Management
2. Finance
3. Sales
4. Production
5. Warehouse
6. Risk management

Answers should be one of the following:

1.	Strongly disagree, no, never	1 point
2.	Somewhat disagree, Seldom	2 points
3.	Somewhat agree, occasionally	3 points
4.	Strongly agree, yes, always, not applicable	4 points

Enter a score of four if any of the questions do not apply to your business.

Do not use this form manually. There is an Excel form that automatically totals your scores for up to twelve participants. Download it at www.leadtosucceed.biz.

Rate your company score as follows:

< 80%	Poor
80% - 84%	Fair
85% - 89%	Good
90% - 100%	Excellent

If you have several of your key managers answer these questions (strongly suggested), make sure that they do not leave any questions unanswered. Either instruct them to call the person who would know the answer or fill in the answer yourself. Any unanswered questions will distort your score. The Excel form will alert you if there are any questions unanswered.

There is a very high correlation between the most successful companies and those scoring over 90 percent overall. Answer these questions objectively and honestly and determine the areas of your company that need improvement. Your goal should be a score of 90 percent or higher in each category.

Management

Question	Score
1. The company has a current organizational chart with all key reporting relationships.	
2. Written job descriptions exist for all positions.	
3. There is an active board of directors, or equivalent, that oversees the affairs of the company.	
4. Key management meets regularly to discuss the operations of the business.	
5. A person is designated with HR responsibilities.	
6. The company has an employee handbook that is reviewed at least annually.	
7. There is a formal indoctrination program for all new hires.	
8. Performance reviews are done on every employee at least annually.	
9. A salary range exists for all positions.	
10. Underachieving employees are counseled and a record is placed in the employee's file.	
11. The company has a vision statement, which is posted prominently.	
12. The company has a mission statement, which is posted prominently.	
13. The company has core values, which are discussed regularly and posted prominently.	
14. The employees are knowledgeable about the vision, mission, and core values.	
15. There is a succession plan in place for all key employees.	
16. The company has key strategic objectives that are determined every year.	
17. The telephone system is up-to-date and sufficient.	
18. The computer hardware is up-to-date and sufficient.	
19. The software programs are up to date and sufficient.	
20. A person is designated with overall IT responsibility.	
21. The company has competitive fringe benefits.	
22. Communications within the company are good.	
23. Suggestions or recommendations are routinely solicited from employees.	
24. There is a system in place for employees to rate their supervisor (upstream evaluation).	
25. The physical appearance of the company is good and well-maintained.	
26. There is a formal program for recognizing important employee anniversaries and achievements.	
27. There is an annual planning process, which involves all key management.	
28. Goals are established for all key managers, and they are held accountable for achieving them.	
29. Key employees have input to major changes that affect them.	
30. Computer files and systems are regularly backed up.	
Total	

Finance

Question	Score
1. The company has annual forecasted income statement, balance sheet, cash flow, and ratios.	
2. The company has an annual capital budget.	
3. Financial statements are prepared no later than twenty days after the end of the month.	
4. Key managers meet at least monthly to go over results versus forecast.	
5. Action is taken on a timely basis if forecasts are not being achieved.	
6. Key managers are held responsible for achieving forecasts in their area.	
7. A person has responsibility for regularly reviewing and collecting past due accounts receivable.	
8. Financial ratios are calculated every month and reviewed and understood by management.	
9. Invoices are issued to all customers promptly.	
10. Adequate checks and balances are in place to ensure against theft or fraud.	
11. Operating and financing cash flow are calculated and monitored regularly.	
12. The bank statement is reconciled monthly.	
13. A person is responsible for bank relations and meets with the banker two to three times a year.	
14. The company has a credit policy, which is understood and followed.	
15. Company credit cards are monitored and audited regularly.	
16. The accounting staff is knowledgeable, well-trained, and sufficient.	
17. The balance sheet is strong, with good liquidity and safety.	
18. The company is sufficiently diversified so that it is profitable in every quarter.	
Total	

Sales

Question	Score
1. The company has established goals for each salesperson.	
2. The company has good sales leadership.	
3. The sales plan supports the income statement forecast.	
4. Actual sales versus goals are reported and reviewed by each salesperson regularly.	
5. The company has good sales support personnel.	
6. Closing ratios are calculated and reviewed with salespeople regularly.	
7. Draws paid to salespersons are monitored to ensure that they are not in excess of commissions earned.	
8. Expense reports are submitted monthly and reviewed by the appropriate person.	
9. Salespeople receive regular training on sales techniques.	
10. Salespeople know the strengths and weaknesses of their primary competitors.	
11. Salespeople are aware of costs and pricing strategies that will produce good profit margins.	
12. The perks given to salespeople are competitive.	
13. The sales manager or CEO occasionally participates in sales calls with salespeople.	
14. Job costing/profitability analysis is performed on a periodic basis.	
15. A formal advertising/marketing plan is developed on an annual basis.	
16. Salespeople have adequate computing equipment.	
17. There is a formal program for gaining referrals from satisfied customers.	
Total	

Production

Question	Score
1. The aisles are kept clear and clean.	
2. All work sites are adequate, orderly, and kept clean.	
3. Inventory is well-secured from theft or shrinkage.	
4. Physical inventory or cycle counts are taken as required.	
5. The OSHA Small Business Checklist is consulted at least twice yearly for compliance.	
6. The local fire department is familiar with the facility and has inspected it within the last year.	
7. Employees are required to dress in appropriate attire at all times.	
8. Adequate security cameras and alarms are in place and operational.	
9. Used material is disposed of or recycled promptly if not reusable.	
10. OSHA Job Safety and Health Protection posters are displayed prominently.	
11. OSHA required Hazard Assessment has been performed and documented.	
12. Appropriate personal protective equipment is available and properly used.	
13. Production employees are trained regularly in the operation of equipment or vehicles.	
14. All signage is clean, well maintained, and attractive.	
15. The production facility is in good condition and well maintained.	
16. Fire doors and exits are well-marked and free of obstructions.	
17. All equipment is well-maintained and adequate for the tasks involved.	
18. No smoking signs are prominently placed and enforced.	
19. All flammable or toxic materials are properly stored.	
20. A log is kept of all work-related injuries or illnesses.	
21. Fire control equipment is regularly inspected and is adequate.	
22. Lighting is well maintained and adequate.	
23. There is a procedure for handling any in-house complaints regarding safety or health issues.	
24. There is an active safety training program with one person designated as responsible for safety.	
25. Adequate medical and first aid equipment is on hand and checked regularly.	
Total	

Warehouse

Question	Score
1. The aisles are kept clear and clean.	
2. Inventory is kept in an orderly fashion and is secured from theft or shrinkage.	
3. Used material is disposed of or recycled promptly if not re-usable.	
4. The yard is kept clean and free of trash.	
5. Warehouse employees are required to be in company uniforms.	
6. Adequate security cameras and alarms are in place and operational.	
7. Warehouse crews are trained regularly in their duties.	
8. All signage is clean, well maintained, and attractive.	
9. The warehouse is in good condition and well maintained.	
10. Access to the warehouse is limited and controlled.	
11. Fire doors and exits are free of obstructions.	
12. All warehouse equipment is well maintained and adequate for tasks involved.	
13. No smoking signs are prominently placed and enforced.	
14. All flammable liquids are properly stored.	
15. Warehouse doors are closed when not in use.	
16. Fire control equipment is regularly inspected and is adequate.	
17. Lighting of warehouse and yard is well maintained and adequate.	
18. Gates and fence are well maintained and adequate for security.	
Total	

Risk Management

Question	Score
1. The company has consulted with an insurance agent experienced in the industry regarding the risks outlined by legal counsel.	
2. The company is adequately covered for liability exposures.	
3. A person is designated as responsible for safety and there is a safety manual.	
4. Regular safety meetings are held with a written agenda and minutes.	
5. The company has an up-to-date written disaster plan in place that is reviewed with all staff.	
6. The risk management program is reviewed regularly by counsel and the insurance agent.	
7. Adequate background checks are conducted on all employees.	
8. Employment applications specifically ask about arrests, convictions, and deferred adjudications.	
9. No drivers are hired with a previous DUI conviction.	
10. No employees are hired with any record of violent crimes.	
11. Employees are terminated if caught bringing drugs, alcohol, or weapons onto company premises or vehicles.	
12. An accident report is filled out for every injury requiring first aid or medical treatment.	
13. Every accident involving personal injury is investigated and written up.	
14. Employees are tested for drugs after every accident.	
15. Appropriate employees are randomly tested for drugs.	
16. Employees have all signed an authorization to allow drug and alcohol testing on both a random and post-accident basis.	
Total	

Make sure you and your key managers take the business review test at least annually. It will allow you to determine the areas in your business that need to be improved. Look especially at areas where you score lower than you expected, and make sure you understand the reasons for this. Prioritize the most important areas and work with your key managers to make needed improvements.

APPENDIX IV

THE "LEFT BEHIND" LIST

What would happen if you stepped in front of a bus tomorrow? What kind of a mess would you leave? The people who are left behind after your passing are going to need to know the following information so sit down and take the time to write it all down. Put it all in a three ring binder and let them know where it is. Keep it up-to-date on at least an annual basis. You will save a lot of trouble for a lot of people, and they will be very grateful.

I. **Personal Information**
    Names, phone numbers, addresses, birthdates and social security numbers for you, your spouse, previous spouses, parents, all living children of you and your spouse, their marital status and all others in your will.

II. **Advisors: phone number and address**
    a. Attorney who drew the will
    b. Corporate attorney
    c. Family business advisory board
    d. Accountant—tax, corporate, and estate planning
    e. Insurance agent
    f. Financial planner
    g. Business consultant
    h. Family advisor
    i. Other

III. **Personal Bank Accounts**
    a. Name of bank(s)
    b. Branch location
    c. Name of primary banker
    d. Signors on the accounts
    e. Type of account (JTWRS, etc.)
    f. Location of safe deposit box, location of key and who is authorized entrance
    g. Documents kept in the safe deposit box
    h. Outstanding credit cards, type, number and PIN

IV. **Documents: indicate location of original, include copy if appropriate**
    a. Will
    b. Tax returns
    c. Gift tax returns
    d. Community property agreement
    e. Durable power of attorney
    f. Living will
    g. Medical power of attorney
    h. Trusts
    i. Pre-nuptial agreement
    j. Divorce decree
    k. Life insurance policies

l. Shareholder agreement

m. Partnership agreement

n. Contracts

o. Notes receivable

p. Notes/mortgages payable

q. Other files and papers along with disposition instructions

V. **Assets—indicate location, how to access information online, passwords, whether joint or separate property, etc.**

a. Stocks, bonds, mutual funds

b. Certificates of deposit

c. 401(k), profit sharing, IRA

d. 529 plans

e. Notes receivable

f. Vehicles: cars, boats, airplanes, RV

g. Real estate: location and legal description

   1. residence
   2. vacation
   3. investment
   4. time-share

h. Corporate interests: percentage owned, other owners

i. Partnership interests: percentage owned, other partners

j. Sole proprietor interest

k. Farm/ranch

l. Other

m. Best guess as to overall value of all assets: $_____

VI. **Liabilities: indicate personal guarantees**

a. Personal mortgages

b. Corporate debt guaranteed

c. Partnership debt

d. Other

e. Current approximate amount of all personal liabilities: $_____

VII. **Life Insurance**

a. Location of policies

b. Amount of death benefit

c. Insured

d. Beneficiaries

e. Total amount of life insurance on you: $_____

f. Total amount of life insurance on spouse: $_____

g. Total amount of second-to-die insurance: $_____

VIII. **Personal Effects**

a. Jewelry

b. Art

c. Collections

d. Antiques

e. Season tickets (sports, theater, symphony, etc.)

f. Mementos

IX. **Personal biographies for you and your spouse.**

Information about you and your life that your heirs may not have and may never have if you don't write it down here. Include anecdotes and recollections about what it was like when you were growing up, key people and memories in your life, activities you were involved in, awards you received, etc. Also include information about your family tree if it is not available elsewhere. If you want, you can even write your own obituary to make sure they get it right!

X. **Personal Wishes**

Aside from the formal dispositions in your will, outline some of the things that you would like your executor or administrator to know about, such as:

a. How you would like your personal effects distributed

b. Who you feel is the most qualified to assume management of the family business and who would be your second choice

c. What you feel is the most desirable disposition of the family business

d. Who you feel should be relied upon for legal, tax and financial advice

e. How you would like your remains disposed of

f. What kind of memorial service you would like

g. The amount of effort used to keep you alive

h. The people to rely upon if you are incapacitated

i. Anything else that comes to your mind that the people left behind should know.

When you have all of this information compiled in a notebook, have a family meeting and go over it. Talk about all aspects of it. Answer all of their questions.

A formal meeting is highly recommended but if you don't want to have one, then simply tell them that you have compiled all of the information that they might need if you and your spouse don't make it back from your next vacation. Those left behind will love you for it.

Caution. This information is sensitive and confidential, and should not be left carelessly lying around. Consider putting it in your safe deposit box if you do not have a secure place to keep it in your home. If you do have it at home, keep it in a fire-proof file, if possible. Storing it in a confidential file on your computer with a backup flash drive in your safe deposit box would be a good alternative.

One final thing: Put a reminder on your calendar to look at this information every year to make sure it is updated and still represents your current thinking and situation. Then go off on your vacation with your spouse, confident that if you don't make it back, those that are *left behind* will be in very good shape. Thanks to you!

APPENDIX V

THE ADVISORY BOARD

I. Membership:
Membership should be in the five to seven range with one or two outside members. Members should be selected for their expertise and their ability and desire to interact with the other participants. They should trust and respect each other and interact well on a personal and business basis. Attendance of the company's attorney or banker is often desirable but it is not advisable to have either as formal members of the advisory board due to conflict of interest issues.

II. Authority:
An advisory board has only the authority given it by the owners of the company. It is not a formal, legal body like the elected board of directors of a corporation. An advisory board's responsibility is to advise, and it does not have the power to bind either management or the corporation unless authorized by ownership. Members should be indemnified by a written hold harmless declaration of the actual board of directors of the company to protect them from personal liability.

III. Compensation:
Normal compensation is $500 to $1,000 per meeting, plus expenses. Meetings usually last four to eight hours, and preparation is required on the part of board members prior to the meeting in the form of reviewing financial information, reports, proposals, etc.

IV. Board Duties:
A. Be knowledgeable about the general operations of the company.
B. Be knowledgeable about the financial operations of the company. Prepare for each meeting by reviewing financial information in advance.
C. Provide input into the hiring and termination of key personnel.
D. Review and approve the annual operating plan.
E. Provide input into compensation of key management and bonus plans.
F. Ask questions, challenge ideas or suggestions and be active rather than passive.
G. Provide input into any disagreements or disputes between key personnel.
H. Assist in the determination of long-term strategic objectives and goals.
I. Assist and provide input into the performance of key personnel.
J. Be available for telephone conferences between meetings, as required.
K. Be knowledgeable about the corporate by-laws and articles of incorporation, and provide oversight to ensure compliance.
L. Be sure to attend all meetings.
M. Exercise utmost good faith and diligence in all corporate matters, and avoid any self-dealing or conflict of interest with the company.
N. Monitor compliance with laws and corporate policies.

V. Frequency of Meetings:

Two to four times per year, following the publication of company's financial statements.

VI. Benefits:

    A. Stimulates the owner's aspirations and confidence about the business.

    B. Raises the expectations, performance, and efficiency of key managers.

    C. Provides a source of objectivity to management, family and company leadership.

    D. Promotes a higher degree of professionalism within the company.

    E. Assists in the objective evaluation of the CEO's performance.

    F. Provides insights in formulating long-term strategy.

    G. Enhances the image of the company in the community.

    H. Acts as a mentor/advisor for the CEO.

    I. Assists in the preparation of a succession plan.

    J. Provides expertise and advice on an affordable basis.

    K. Allows for continuity of the business in the event of an unexpected loss of the CEO or owner.

VII. Disadvantages:

    A. Adds to the work of the CEO and key management in preparing reports.

    B. Can slow decision making at times.

    C. Board expense.

    D. Possible expense of errors and omissions insurance.

VIII. Potential Agenda:

    I. General Session: Advisory board plus key managers and CFO.

        A. Approval of minutes of the prior meeting.

        B. CEO's report:

            1. Actual performance vs. goals.

            2. Questions or concerns.

            3. Capital expenditures for next quarter.

        C. Presentation of financial statements—CFO.

        D. Cash flow report and forecast—CFO.

        E. Sales/marketing report—sales manager.

        F. Operations report—operations manager.

        G. Production report—production manager.

        H. Confirmation of future meeting dates.

    II. Executive session—advisory board members only:

        A. Personnel issues.

        B. Performance evaluation.

        C. Compensation issues.

        D. Other sensitive company matters.

APPENDIX VI

SOFTWARE AND FORMS

The following software and forms are available at www.leadtosucceed.biz

SOFTWARE

Financial analysis—— calculates ratios and cash flow after you input your data.
Break-even—calculates break-even sales after you input your fixed and variable expenses.
Business review—allows up to twelve people to score your company and automatically calculates percentages for each area and the overall company.
Capital budgeting—calculates net present value after you input your data.

FORMS

Ratio worksheet
Cash flow worksheet
Break-even worksheet
Employee satisfaction index
Upstream evaluation
The Left Behind List

GLOSSARY

Accounts payable
A current liability representing the amount owed to trade creditors for merchandise or services purchased on open account (i.e., without giving a note or other evidence of debt).

Accounts payable period (days)
Expressed in days, it represents the length of time it typically takes to pay trade creditors. This is calculated by dividing cost of goods sold by accounts payable, which is equal to accounts payable turnover, and then dividing 365 by this turnover. If the period being measured is not a year, then cost of goods sold should be annualized before making this calculation.

Accounts receivable
A current asset representing money owed for merchandise or services sold on open account.

Accounts receivable aging
Grouping accounts receivable according to due dates that represent the length of time an account has been outstanding, such as:
> 0–30 days
> 31–60 days
> 61–90 days
> Over 90 days

Accounts receivable collection period (also known as days sales outstanding or DSO)
Expressed in days, it represents the length of time it typically takes to collect outstanding accounts receivable. This is calculated by dividing sales by accounts receivable, which is equal to accounts receivable turnover, and then dividing 365 by this turnover. If the period being measured is not a year, then sales should be annualized before making this calculation.

Accrual-basis accounting
The practice of record keeping by which sales is recorded when earned, and expenses are recorded when incurred, even though cash may not be received or paid out until later. This is opposed to cash-basis accounting, which only recognizes sales when cash is received, or expenses when cash is paid.

Accrued expenses
A current liability representing expenses incurred during a fiscal period, but not actually paid by the end of that fiscal period.

Accumulated depreciation
Also referred to as allowance or reserve for depreciation. The total of all depreciation taken on a fixed asset since its purchase.

Administrative expenses
Also referred to as general and administrative expenses (G&A), operating expenses, indirect expenses, or overhead. These expenses typically include utilities, advertising, legal, accounting, travel, entertainment, administrative salaries, office expenses, professional fees, taxes and licenses, etc.

Amortization expense
The gradual write-off of an intangible asset, such as copyright or goodwill, over a period of years. It is a noncash charge against earnings, similar to depreciation.

Appreciation
The increase in the value of an asset in excess of its cost or book value, which is due to economic and other conditions.

Asset
Anything owned by an individual or a business. Assets may consist of specific property or claims against others. Assets are reflected on the balance sheet at the lower of cost or current value.

Bad debts
The amounts due on open accounts that have been proven uncollectible.

Balance sheet
An itemized statement of all of the assets, liabilities, and equity of an individual or business at a given point in time. It is known as a position statement.

Balance sheet spread
The organization of several years of balance sheets on one piece of paper for ease of analysis of trends and calculation of financial ratios.

Book value
The value of the assets, liabilities, and equity as reflected on the balance sheet. The book value of a business is determined by deducting total liabilities from total assets. Book value of the assets of a company may have little or no relationship to the actual fair market value of the assets.

Break-even point
The point at which sales and expenses are equal. A combination of sales and expenses that will yield zero net profit.

Budget
An itemized listing of the amount of all estimated sales that a given business anticipates receiving and the listing and segregation of the amount of all estimated expenses that will be incurred in obtaining the income during a given period of time, such as a month, a year, etc.

Capital
The amount of money invested in the business by shareholders. It consists of the initial stock investment and retained earnings It is also referred to as equity or net worth.

Capital assets
A term that includes all fixed assets, consisting of vehicles, furniture and fixtures, land, buildings, machinery, etc.

Capital budgeting
The practice of allocating funds set aside for investment in fixed assets in the most effective manner. It takes into consideration the risks and possible returns of various potential investments. It is the process of determining whether or not an asset should be purchased based upon its estimated generated cash flows. It is the process of planning expenditures for capital (fixed) assets.

Capital gain or loss
The gain or loss between the book value and sale price of a capital (fixed) asset.

Capital stock
The shares of a corporation authorized by its articles of incorporation, including preferred and common stocks.

Cash-basis accounting
The practice of recording income and expenses only when cash is actually received or paid out. This is opposed to accrual-basis accounting, which recognizes sales when items or services are sold and expenses when they are incurred, versus when they are paid.

Cash budget
A schedule forecasting of cash inflows and cash outflows over a specified period of time.

Cash flow
This term may have different meanings, depending upon who is using the term and in what context. Bankers usually define it as net profit plus all noncash expenses (depreciation and amortization), but it can also be defined as the difference between cash receipts and disbursements over a specified period of time. This text describes operating cash flow and financing cash flow, which differ slightly from the definitions applied by a CPA in their statement of cash flow as provided with CPA-prepared financial statements.

Collateral
Assets that secure a loan.

Common-sized balance sheet or income statement
The process of dividing individual sales and expense account balances by total sales or dividing an individual asset, liability, or equity account by total assets to determine each account's value as a percentage of sales or total assets. For the balance sheet, each account is divided by total assets. For the income statement, each account is divided by sales/revenue.

Comprehensive financial plan
A comprehensive financial plan is comprised of an historical review and a three-year projection of the income statement, balance sheet, cash flow, and financial ratios.

Contribution margin
The difference between sales and variable expenses:

sales	$400,000
minus variable expenses	($150,000)
equals contribution margin	$250,000

This tells you that you have $250,000 left after paying variable expenses to pay fixed expenses. If your fixed expenses exceed $250,000, then you need to either increase sales or reduce fixed expenses, or both, in order to avoid losing money.

Contribution margin ratio (CMR)
The contribution margin expressed as a percentage of sales.

sales ÷ contribution margin = contribution margin ratio.

Corporation
A type of business organization chartered by a state and given legal rights as a separate entity. A C corporation is a tax-paying entity, and an S corporation is not a tax-paying entity but passes its profits (or losses) through to its shareholders.

Cost of goods sold
Expenses related directly to the production of sales for a business. This usually includes raw materials, direct labor, freight, and factory overhead for a manufacturing company; merchandise costs for a wholesaler or retailer; and direct labor and materials for a service company. This is also referred to as direct expenses for a service company.

Current assets
Current assets are those assets of a company that are reasonably expected to be converted to cash or consumed during the next twelve months from the date of the balance sheet. Current assets include cash, accounts receivable, inventories, and prepaid expenses (note that accounts receivable and prepaid expenses exist only on an accrual-basis balance sheet).

Current liabilities
Liabilities that are due within twelve months of the date of the balance sheet. Current liabilities include such accounts as bank line of credit, accrued liabilities, accounts payable, and current portion of long-term debt (note that accounts payable and accrued expenses exist only on an accrual-basis balance sheet).

Current ratio
This ratio is a measure of liquidity and the company's ability to pay its bills. It is calculated by dividing current assets by current liabilities.

Debt-to-equity ratio

This ratio is a measure of the company's safety and ability to survive adversity. It is calculated by dividing total liabilities by equity. This is an important ratio for banks, since it is one way to measure a company's risk level.

Depreciation expense

The amount of expense a company charges against earnings to write off the cost of fixed assets over their useful lives. If the expense is assumed to be incurred in equal amounts in each business period over the life of the asset, the depreciation method used is straight line (SL). If the expense is assumed to be front-loaded and incurred in decreasing amounts in each business period over the life of the asset, the method used is accelerated. Usually straight line depreciation is chosen for financial statement purposes, and accelerated depreciation is chosen for tax return purposes. This produces a lower profit on the tax return and is permitted by IRS regulations.

Direct expenses

This is the same as cost of goods sold. Usually used in reference to a service type business.

Dividend

That portion of a corporation's earnings that is paid to the stockholders and not retained in the business.

Entrepreneur

A person who assumes the risk of starting a business.

Equity

The net worth or ownership interest in a company. It is the difference between the assets and the liabilities of a company. In a corporation, net worth or owner's equity consists of capital stock, capital surplus, and retained earnings.

Financial gap

The financial gap represents the amount of funding the business is unable to generate internally to purchase the assets required to support sales. The business will have to make up the difference with either debt or additional equity.

Fixed assets

Those assets of a noncurrent nature, which will not normally be converted into cash during the next twelve months (which are current assets). Examples are furniture and fixtures, land, buildings, and equipment. A fixed asset that is to be sold within a twelve month time period is not considered to be a current asset.

Fixed expenses

Those expenses that do not vary directly with sales or revenue. Examples include rent, depreciation, lease expense, office expenses, legal, and accounting.

Fluctuating current assets
Those assets that go up and down with seasonal fluctuations in sales. Typically, they are the seasonal demands for inventory and accounts receivable.

Goodwill
Goodwill is an intangible asset that is created to the extent that the purchase price of a company is greater than the fair market value of the total assets. It is synonymous with the term blue sky, and it can only arise on a balance sheet as the result of purchasing a business. Treatment of goodwill for tax or accounting purposes changes from time to time, and it is therefore necessary to ask your CPA how it should be handled.

Gross profit
The difference between sales and the cost of goods sold.

$1,500,000	sales
($975,000)	minus cost of goods sold (direct expenses)
$525,000	equals gross profit

This tells you that you have $525,000 in gross profit to pay overhead or indirect expenses. If your overhead exceeds $525,000, then you either need to increase your gross profit margin, reduce overhead, or both.

Gross profit margin (GPM)
The gross profit expressed as a percentage of sales.

Sales ÷ gross profit = gross profit margin

A gross profit margin of 35 percent would mean that there is $0.35 in gross profit for every $1.00 in sales.

Income statement
The statement of sales, expenses, and profit for a particular period of time. It is known as a period statement.

Indirect expense
Same as operating expense, general and administrative expense (G&A) or overhead. Usually used in reference to a service-type business.

Intangible assets
Nonphysical assets such as goodwill, patents, copyrights, operating authorities, and trademarks.

Inventory turnover
The number of times a business turns its inventory over during the year. This is calculated by dividing cost of goods sold by inventory.

Liabilities
Amounts owed to creditors by a person or a business.

Limited liability company (LLC)

A form of business, similar to a corporation, with liability protection for all of the owners (referred to as members). It is taxed in the same fashion as an S corporation.

Line of credit

An agreement whereby a bank agrees to lend a customer funds up to agreed maximum amount. A line of credit is typically used for seasonal needs to finance inventory and/or accounts receivable and is secured by accounts receivable that do not exceed ninety days.

Liquidity

A term to describe a firm's ability to meet its current obligations. It is measured by the current ratio.

Long-term debt

Liabilities that are due more than one year from the date of the balance sheet.

Markup

The difference between the cost and selling prices of merchandise, usually expressed as a percentage. To calculate markup as a percentage, use the difference between the cost and selling prices for the numerator and the cost for the denominator. An item that cost $1.00 and had a selling price of $1.50 would have a 50 percent markup ($0.50 ÷ $1.00). This is not the same as, but is often confused with, the gross profit margin. In the above example, the gross profit margin would be thirty-three percent (.50 ÷ 1.50). Markup is applied to the cost and gross profit margin is applied to the sales price.

Mortgage

A long-term debt with real estate pledged as collateral.

Net income

Often used by CPAs to signify net profit after tax.

Net loss

The excess of total expenses over total income for a fiscal period, either before or after tax.

Net present value (NPV)

The net present value is equal to the present value of future returns, minus the present value of future payments.

Net profit

The excess of total income over the total expenses for a fiscal period, before income taxes.

Net profit margin

The net profit (before tax) as expressed as a percentage of sales.

> net profit ÷ sales equals net profit margin.

Note payable
A written promise to a person or business to pay a certain amount at a certain time.

Operating cash flow
The cash flow the company generates from its day-to-day operations. The description of operating cash flow in chapter eight is slightly different from the one provided by a CPA-prepared statement of cash flow.

Operating expenses
Those expenses pertaining to the normal operation of the business. Interest expense and nonrecurring losses are not included as operating expenses. Also referred to as overhead or indirect expense.

Operating profit
The difference between the gross profit and overhead or indirect expenses. This tells you the amount of profit that has been generated from operations of your business.

Sales	$950,000
Cost of goods sold	500,000
Gross profit	450,000
Overhead expenses	400,000
Operating profit	50,000

Operating profit margin
The operating profit expressed as a percentage of sales.
Operating profit ÷ sales equals operating profit margin (OPM).
$50,000 ÷ 950,000 = 5.3\%$

Permanent current assets
Represents the permanent base of current assets (inventory, accounts receivable, and cash) that a business will have on hand based on the sales level of the business at its lowest period. In other words, current assets do not go down to zero, and the lowest amount during the year represents the amount of permanent current assets that the business will have.

Preferred stock
Stock that grants its owners certain preference rights over common stockholders, usually dividend and/or voting rights.

Present value
The value today of a future receipt or payment of money, discounted at an appropriate discount rate. The present value of an amount to be received in the future is worth less than the future face amount because of the need to wait for the payment, thus preventing you from earning any return (like interest) on it. Receiving $1.00 in one year's time is the same as a present value of $0.95 if it is discounted at 5 percent. In other words, if you had $0.95 today, it would be worth $1.00 in a year if it were invested at 5 percent. Net present value is the difference between the present value of future receipts and the present value of future payments.

Quick assets
Cash, accounts receivable, and marketable securities.

Quick ratio
The quick ratio is calculated by dividing quick assets by current liabilities. This ratio is not typically calculated for service businesses because it will be very similar to the current ratio.

Retained earnings
Earnings of the business that have been retained in the business and not paid out to stockholders.

Return on assets (ROA)
Return on assets is the ratio of net profit (before taxes) to total assets.
Net profit ÷ total assets = return on assets

Return on equity (ROE)
Return on equity is the ratio of net profit (before taxes) to equity or net worth. This may also be referred to as return on investment (ROI).
Net profit ÷ equity = return on equity

Revenue
Synonymous with sales. Usually used in a service business.

Sales to assets ratio
This is the ratio of sales or revenue divided by total assets.
Sales ÷ total assets = sales to assets ratio

Sales to net fixed assets ratio
This is the ratio of sales or revenue divided by net fixed assets.
Sales ÷ net fixed assets = sales to net fixed assets ratio

Secured loan
A loan that is secured by some sort of collateral, as opposed to an unsecured loan. Secured loans may be either long-term or short-term loans.

Self-liquidating loan
A short-term commercial loan, usually supported by a lien on a given product or commodity, which is liquidated from the proceeds of the sale of the product or commodity.

Stockholder
A person owning shares of the capital stock of a corporation. Also referred to as a shareholder.

Term loan
A long-term loan due in excess of one year.

Trend analysis

The process of measuring financial data over a given time period to note any significant changes in performance from period to period.

Variable assets

Those assets that go up or down with sales or revenue volume, such as accounts receivable. These assets are needed to support sales.

Variable expenses

Expenses that are caused by sales, and go up or down with sales or revenue volume. Examples include commissions, direct wages, supplies, and bad debts.

Variable liabilities

Those liabilities that go up or down with sales volume. They typically are accounts payable and accrued expenses.

Working capital

This is defined as current assets minus current liabilities. All financially stable companies need adequate working capital so that they can make payments when they are due, either to vendors, employees, or creditors. A current ratio of 2.00 means that there is $2.00 in current assets to pay every $1.00 in current liabilities, or $1.00 in working capital ($2.00 minus $1.00).

BIBLIOGRAPHY

Alexander, Caroline, *The Endurance—Shackleton's Legendary Antarctic Expedition*, Alfred A. Knopf, Inc., 2001.

Arrendondo, Lani, *Communicating Effectively*, McGraw-Hill, 2000.

Bennis, Warren, Spreitzer, Gretchen, Cummings, Thomas, *The Future of Leadership*, Jossey-Bass, 2001.

Carlock, Randel, Ward, John, *Strategic Planning for the Family Business*, Palgrave, 2001.

Collins, Jim, *Good to Great*, HarperCollins, 2001.

Covey, Stephen, *Principled-Centered Leadership*, Simon & Schuster, 1992.

Duryee, David A., *Lead to Succeed, the Moving and Storage Guide to Management and Finance*, printed by CreateSpace, an Amazon.com company, 2015.

Duryee, David A., *The Business Owner's Guide to Achieving Financial Success*, Richard D. Irwin, Inc., 1994.

Gerber, Michael E., *The E Myth Revisited*, Harper Collins, Inc. 1995.

Hoffman, Bryce, *American Icon: Alan Mulally and the Fight to Save Ford Motor Company*, Crown Publishing Group, 2012.

Isaacson, Walter, *Steve Jobs*, Simon & Shuster, 2011.

Jaffe, Dennis, *Working with the Ones You Love: Strategies for a Successful Family Business*, Dennis T. Jaffe, 1991.

Julien, Scott M., *What Every Leader Needs to Know: 7 Essential Leadership Secrets*, printed by CreateSpace, an Amazon.com company, 2009.

Le Van, Gerald, *The Survival Guide for Business Families*, Rutledge, 1999.

Posner, Barry, Kouzes, James, *The Leadership Challenge*, Jossey Bass, 1997.

Stack, Jack, *The Great Game of Business*, Bantam Doubleday Dell Publishing Group, Inc. 1992.

Ward, John, *Perpetuating the Family Business*, Palgrave MacMillan, 2004.

ACKNOWLEDGEMENTS

I would be remiss if I did not acknowledge and thank the dozens of CEOs who have freely shared their information and knowledge with me over the last thirty-five years and allowed me to enjoy an intimate look at their operations. As a result, I have developed valuable insights into the leadership qualities of successful business owners. It has been a wonderful and enjoyable learning experience for me.

I have the utmost admiration and respect for business owners who are students of the game, and strive every day to learn and grow and be better in their roles as CEOs and business leaders. This is a tough and demanding position, and only those that diligently work at it and follow the tenets of this book are the ones who consistently excel.

A special thanks to those that helped me so much with the planning, editing and design of this book. Allen Hopson generously designed and developed the software that is available for this book. Claudeen Lyle, Sabrina Jones, Keven St. George, Brandt Allen, Art King, John Colosimo, Chuck Feinstein and Allen Hopson spent many hours going over this manuscript and provided me with invaluable corrections, insights and suggestions. My daughter, Tracy Bech, designed the website and all the art work.

You have all made this a much better book because of your generous help, and I am truly indebted to you all.

AUTHOR'S NOTE

Julian and Allen are real people as are their wives, Sara and Debbie. They are father and son and have graciously agreed to allow me to use their names in this book. Julian did retire to Florida and pass on the business to Allen as the successor CEO.

The rest of the story, however, is complete fiction. Allen managed the company just like dad, in a careful, effective, profitable manner, and with great integrity.

My narrative regarding Durson Distributors is not really all fiction. It is a composite of many companies that I have observed over the years. Conflicts between generations are inevitable, and it is not easy to pass a business successfully on to the next generation, and few do. Conservative mom and dad are bound to clash with hard charging son or daughter on the best course of action for the business. The goal of them all should be to get into the thunder phase of business *and stay there*.

It is easier said than done. Good communication and careful attention to the tenets of this book are the key to making it happen.

Success isn't pre-destined, it's earned. Leaders are not born, they are made. It's hard work, but if you are persistent and diligent, you and your leadership team will be successful and attain *perpetual profitability*.

ABOUT THE AUTHOR

David A. Duryee is the managing director of Horizon Management Services LLC, and has been active in business consulting, succession planning and financial training for over forty years. He received his BA and MBA in finance from the University of Washington and is an honors graduate from the Pacific Coast Banking School. He was a banker for sixteen years, serving initially as a lending officer and subsequently as a trust officer as a vice president and manager of corporate management services. After a sixteen year banking career, he co-owned and operated his own consulting firm and subsequently managed the valuation services division for a large west-coast CPA firm. Mr. Duryee served in the U.S. Army, achieving the rank of Captain as an artillery battery commander, and was awarded the Army Commendation Medal for outstanding leadership.

In addition to this book, Mr. Duryee is the author or co-author of several books, including *Lead to Succeed—the Moving and Storage Guide to Management and Finance*, *The Business Owner's Guide to Achieving Financial Success*, *A Dealer Guide to Valuing an Automobile Dealership*, *A Dealer Guide to Financial Management*, *A Dealer Guide to Succession Planning* and *Small Business Banking, Assessing Needs and Establishing Strategies*, as well as numerous articles in trade publications. He is a nationally known lecturer to business owners, bankers, and professionals, and sits on the advisory boards of several corporations.

Mr. Duryee divides his time between Rancho Mirage, California, and Seattle, Washington.

He can be reached at dave@leadtosucceed.biz.

Software and forms for this book can be obtained and downloaded at no charge from www.leadtosucceed.biz.

Keep on paddling!

25545882R00115

Made in the USA
San Bernardino, CA
03 November 2015